P9-CDC-700

2,00

150
YEARS OF
NORTH AMERICAN
RAILROADS

BERNARD FITZSIMONS

CHARTWELL BOOKS, INC.

Copyright © 1982 Winchmore Publishing Services
Limited.

All rights reserved. No part of this publication may be
reproduced or transmitted, in any form, or by any
means, without permission from the Publisher.

Printed in Hong Kong

First published in the United States by

Chartwell Books Inc.
A division of Book Sales Inc.
110 Enterprise Avenue,
Secaucus, New Jersey 07094.

ISBN: 0 89009 534 5

Produced by Winchmore Publishing Services Limited.
48 Lancaster Avenue,
Hadley Wood, Herts.

Edited by Leslie Berstein Editorial Services
Designed by Pierre Tilley and Andrzej Bielecki
Picture Research by Jonathan and Diane Moore
House Editor John Gilbert

CONTENTS

FIRST RAILS AND FALSE STARTS

By the beginning of the nineteenth century, with independence won and the Indians largely subdued, the great tide of western movement across the North American continent was gaining momentum. High taxes, rising land prices and a rigid social order along the Atlantic coast, compounded in the southern states by soil exhaustion and the spread of plantation agriculture, provided the motivation for hundreds of thousands of Americans to head for the interior.

The routes they followed were the new roads – at that stage little more than tracks hacked through the under-growth – that led west from Boston and New England along the Mohawk valley to Lake Erie, from Philadelphia and Baltimore across the Appalachians to the Ohio River valley, and from Virginia and North Carolina to Nashville and Louisville. Thereafter the rivers provided the main communications, and in the first quarter of the century new routes appeared. The paved National Road was completed to Wheeling, on the Ohio River, by 1818, and in 1825 the Erie Canal was opened between the Hudson River and Lake Erie across northern New York. From the south the fertile plains of Ohio, Indiana and

The ceremony held to mark the official start of building the Baltimore and Ohio, on July 4, 1828.

Illinois were being penetrated by the first paddle steamers.

The result of this movement was the cultivation of vast new areas of land and the creation of huge surpluses of grain and other produce, just as the first factories were introducing industrialization to the northeastern states and the south was turning increasingly to cotton production. The merchants of the east coast cities could see their future in the exchange of food from the interior

The B and O locomotive *Atlantic* in a symbolic scene showing the rivalry between the canals and railroads.

for their manufactured goods: the only problem was transport. The roads across the mountains were too slow for large-scale transportation of grain, while the river routes south to New Orleans, and the subsequent sea journey from the Gulf of Mexico to the eastern ports were not only slow and tortuous but also encountered climatic conditions which were potentially damaging to the merchandise.

The Erie Canal proved to be the first breakthrough, making possible dramatic reductions in both the cost of transport and the time taken. A direct consequence of its success was the establishment of New York as the leading center for trade, and this in turn provoked the other northeastern ports to seek their own connections with the interior.

The immediate clamor was for canals, but the formidable difficulties of driving canals through the intervening mountains proved all but overwhelming. Philadelphia devised, and persuaded the state of Pennsylvania to build, a system of canals which by 1834 reached as far as Pittsburgh; but in order to cross the mountain ridge goods had to be hauled ten miles up a series of inclined planes and coasted down the other side before continuing their journey.

Another canal, the Chesapeake and Ohio, was begun in 1827 under the joint sponsorship of Baltimore and Washington, D.C., but the same year saw the foundation of an entirely new enterprise that was to overshadow the canal and revolutionize transport. This was the Baltimore and Ohio Railroad, chartered by the state of Maryland on February 28, 1827, and inspired by reports of steam engines in England that traveled at speeds three and four times the 4 mph that was the best the canals could offer. From Baltimore to the Ohio River, where the rails would link up with the river network that carried most of the trade in the interior, was 380 miles across an imposing mountain range, well over ten times the length of any railroad previously attempted; but despite a general lack of railroad-building experience the scheme was pursued with a vigor to match its ambition.

Army engineers called in to conduct a survey chose a route that started off along the Patapsco River, before cutting across country to follow the Potomac through the Caboctin mountains. Work was begun on July 4, 1828, and within three years profits from horse-drawn traffic on the first few miles of track encouraged the B. & O.'s directors to take a bold new step. In 1831 prizes of $4000 and $3500 were offered for the best steam locomotives delivered by June 1 that year: the engines were not to weigh more than three and a half tons, and must be capable of pulling a 15 ton train at 15 mph.

By this stage a number of steam locomotives had appeared in the United States. The first was a little engine built by an early American advocate of railroads, Colonel John Stevens, and demonstrated on a small track in his garden. The first commercial models, however, were imported from England, ordered by Horatio Allen on behalf of the Delaware and Hudson Canal company. The D & H was building a canal from Rondout, New York, to the Carbondale mines in northwestern Pennsylvania, when the difficulties of building through the last 16 miles from Honesdale led company engineer John B. Jervis to investigate the possibility of substituting a railroad. Allen was sent to England to buy iron rails and any locomotives he considered suitable; the first of them, *America*, built by Robert Stephenson, arrived in New York in January, 1829.

Another three locomotives were ordered from the Stourbridge firm of Foster, Rastrick, and although two of these, *Hudson* and *Delaware*, were destroyed by fire in the shed where they were stored after their arrival at Rondout, the *Stourbridge Lion*, having been tested at the West Point Foundry in New York City following its arrival in

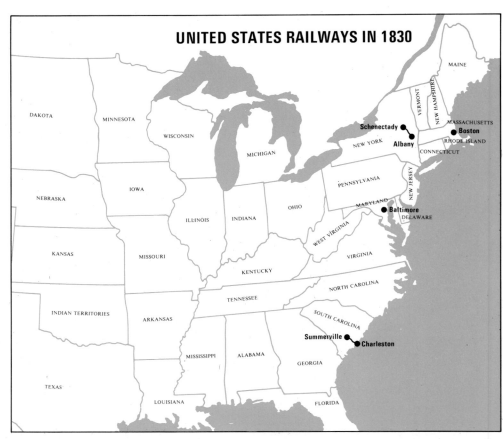

UNITED STATES RAILWAYS IN 1830

By 1830 railroads were being built westward from Boston, Albany, Baltimore and Charleston. Early operation was by horse traction, as recreated (below) outside the Baltimore and Ohio's original station and old engine shed, now a museum, at Mount Clare, with a reconstruction of Peter Cooper's experimental locomotive *Tom Thumb*. The illustration opposite shows *Tom Thumb* overshadowed by the ghostly outlines of one of the 80-mph President class locomotives built for the B&O's new through service between Washington and Jersey City in 1927. First locomotive run in America was made by the Delaware and Hudson Canal's *Stourbridge Lion* (opposite, below).

May 1829, was shipped to Honesdale. On August 8 the *Lion* was prepared for its first trip, and in view of the warped wooden rails and twisting course of the track, Allen took the footplate alone. Setting off boldly, Allen and his new engine rattled along the 500-ft straight that preceded a sharp curve leading onto a trestle bridge. Defying predictions of disaster, the *Lion* negotiated the curve, crossed the bridge, and after a three-mile spin through the woods returned safely to its starting point to complete the first locomotive journey in America.

Allen may have been lucky. The subsequent career of the *Lion* was marked by frequent derailments, and it was relegated to service as a stationary boiler in a Carbondale foundry, though rebuilt for the Chicago Railway Exposition of 1884 and ultimately preserved by the Smithsonian Institution.

The Baltimore and Ohio, meanwhile, had begun operations, and in 1830 one of its shareholders, Peter Cooper, built his own locomotive. Designed merely as a demonstration model, Cooper's *Tom Thumb* weighed only one ton, used gun barrels for boiler tubes and incorporated a fan driven by one of the axles to provide draft for the fire. Nevertheless, on August 28, 1830, *Tom Thumb* pulled a coach carrying 36 passengers along the 15 miles of track from Baltimore to Ellicott's Mills at speeds up to 18 mph. On the return journey a horse-drawn railcar on the parallel track challenged Cooper to a race, and was convincingly outpaced before the belt to the blower fan slipped, the fire died, and the horse car was left to come home alone.

Cooper, however, had made his point. The winner of the resulting competition, and the only entry to meet the conditions, was the *York*, designed by Phineas Davis, a Philadelphia watchmaker. The B & O ordered 20 improved models, and these 'grasshopper' engines, with vertical boilers driving the wheels through rocking beams, proved capable of pulling 50-ton trains on the railroad's winding track. Many remained at work for up to 50 years, and the last was not retired until 1893.

Already other firms were experimenting with locomotives. In 1830 the *Best Friend of Charleston* was built by the

STOURBRIDGE LION.

The vast distances and rugged terrain with which the western railroads had to contend called for ingenuity and adaptability on the part of builders and operators. Overleaf, a snow-clearing gang pose with their equipment on the Northern Pacific in 1886. The Denver and Rio Grande adopted a gauge of 3 ft for its original lines in the Rockies, as on this section (left) in 1875. The Milwaukee Road turned to electrification for its mountain sections: here three electric locomotives head a heavy freight out of Harlowton, Montana.

The second failure ousted Villard for good, and by 1896 Hill had gained control of the parallel route. But even with two transcontinental railroads under his control he was not satisfied: his ambition now was to expand into Chicago and the Midwest.

There were two possible means to this end. The Chicago, Burlington and Quincy Railroad was formed in 1856 by the amalgamation of a couple of small lines in the Chicago area, and over the years it had grown by extensions and takeovers into a system of over 6000 route miles reaching from Chicago as far afield as St Louis, Kansas City and Denver, north to Minneapolis and northwest into Montana. The other system that would have answered Hill's needs, the Chicago, Milwaukee and St Paul, had the backing of Standard Oil founder William Rockefeller, and was not for sale; so the Chicago, Burlington and Quincy was added to Hill's empire.

By this time the term 'transcontinental' had lost much of its meaning. There was no through line from the Atlantic to the Pacific, although one man did almost bring it about a decade or so later. This was George Gould, heir to the Mephistopheles of Wall Street. Until the panic of 1907 Gould had included the Denver and Rio Grande Western, the Wabash and the Western Maryland among his extensive railroad interests; and when his Western Pacific was completed in 1909 between Ogden, Iowa, and San Francisco, he came close to achieving a system that actually did span the continent from coast to coast.

The transcontinentals were by no means the be-all and end-all of railroading in the west. Railroads were built wherever there was a need, and often where there was none, as the old frontier was tamed and disappeared under the advancing rails. In the Colorado Rockies, for example, the Denver and Rio Grande was only one, albeit by far the biggest, of several railroads serving the mining towns of the area. Much of the D & RG's track was originally built to the 3-ft gauge that became popular in the west after 1870, although narrow-gauge railroads always had the disadvantage of being unable to exchange traffic with standard-gauge lines. The Rio Grande soon began to convert most of its track to standard gauge, though

the narrow-gauge branch from Durango to Silverton was preserved as a tourist attraction, and steam-hauled excursion trains have continued to be operated over that branch.

There was, however, one transcontinental line still to be built, one which epitomized the wastefulness of much nineteenth-century construction in that it competed directly with two existing systems, yet which in its operation was to become one of the most advanced in the country.

As outlined above, James Hill had been baulked in his attempt to acquire the Chicago, Milwaukee and St Paul Railroad to complement his twin Great Northern and Northern Pacific transcontinental routes, but had succeeded in gaining control of the Chicago, Burlington and Quincy. The reaction of the Milwaukee road's management was a decision, taken in 1905, to build its own northwestern road to the Pacific. With none of the land grants that had helped its predecessors complete their lines, the Milwaukee nevertheless built its line in the remarkably short space of three years, and over a route shorter than either of its competitors, between Chicago and Seattle.

This was only achieved at considerable expense, and by following a route that included some very severe grades through a series of mountain ranges. As a result of the operational difficulties and challenges, the Milwaukee, which now added the word Pacific to its full title but which became known universally as the Milwaukee Road, was induced to embark on an ambitious electrification scheme in the Rocky and Bitter Root Mountains. Two sections were equipped with overhead supply of 3000-volt DC current, that between Harlowtown and Avery being opened in 1917 and the other, from Othello to Seattle, in 1920. Together they represented 656 miles of electrified main line, the longest in the world at the time and using the most advanced system available. The eventual replacement of steam power by diesel locomotives, and the inconvenience of the 110-mile gap between the two electrified sections, led the Milwaukee to decide, in 1973, to abandon its electric operations, which had proved a thoroughly economic exercise.

53

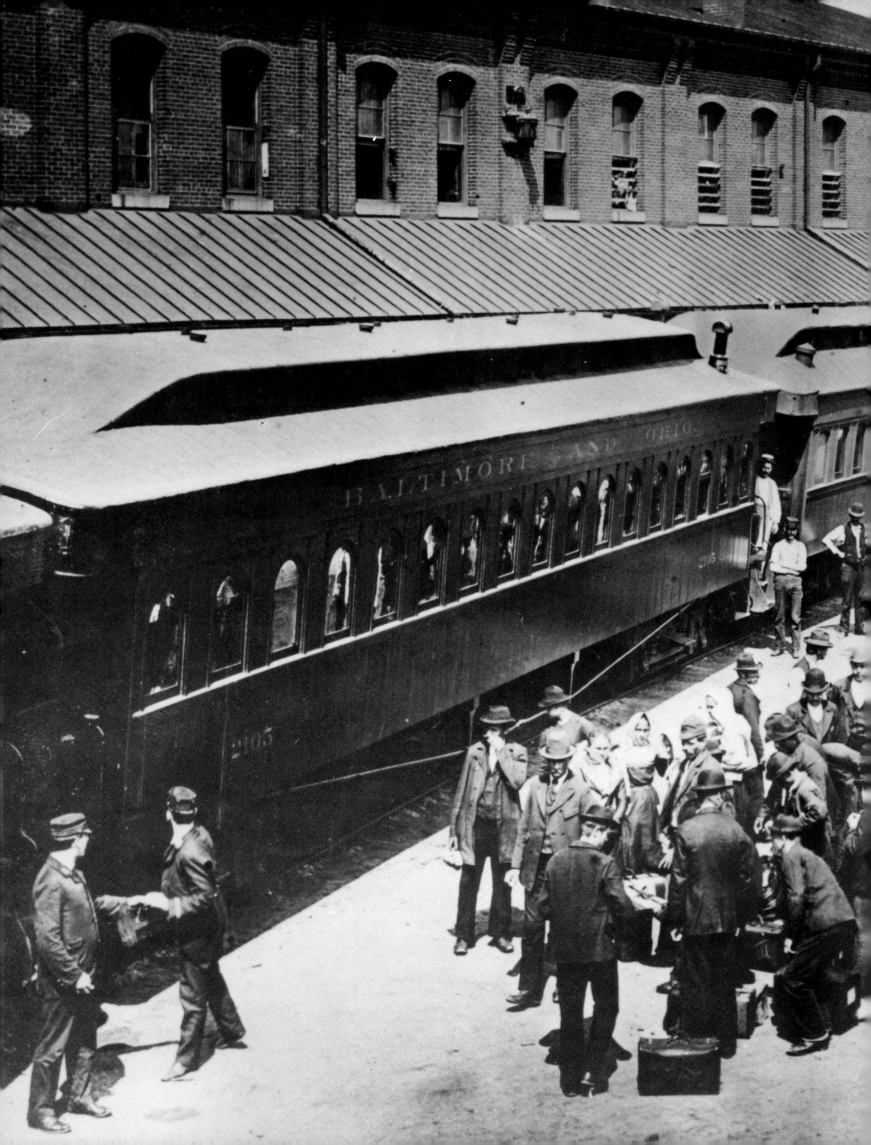

REGULATING THE RAILROADS

The major railroads and the sorry catalog of scandals that blackened their name, only constituted part of the story. There were, in fact, railroads of every size, from the massive systems that measured their extent in thousands of miles to single-track lines a few miles long and operated by a single locomotive; there were specialized freight operators concentrating on a single product – coal, mineral ore, chemicals or lumber; and there were suburban railroads catering almost exclusively for commuters. But it was clear that, whatever their individual forms, the railroads as a whole had become too important to be left to the vagaries of market forces and the whims of tycoons.

Many of the troubles that beset the railroads were a consequence of their origins. Before the Civil War railroads were chartered by individual states, which could have important effects on their routes. The Erie, for example, followed a route across southern New York that was governed more by the location of the state line than by any more practical consideration. The Congressional land grant system, applied first to the transcontinental railroads and later to new railroads in the Territories, produced systems that were dependent on through traffic, rather than local demand, and this in turn tended toward consolidation of individual roads into interstate systems.

At first this process was left entirely to the initiative of individual managements, and the results were largely dependent on their characters. Thus the Pennsylvania Railroad, under the presidency of J. Edgar Thompson and his successor, Thomas A. Scott, became the premier system of the world, the standard against which all others were measured: its track was the finest, its locomotives outstanding, its services so impressive that Henry James, returning to the United States in 1904 after twenty years in Europe, was moved to single it out for special praise. In *The American Scene* James recorded his impression that the Pennsylvania was actually designed to serve another

Austere elegance in the dining car of the Great Northern Railroad's Oriental Limited in about 1910.

57

world, and that by staying on board beyond his destination he might be carried to some ideal city not mentioned in any timetable, passengers being merely a vulgar intrusion on its more sublime operations.

Allowing for such fanciful exaggeration, there is no doubt that other systems existed which, to say the least, compared unfavorably with the Penn. The nature of the competition between the railroads that arose from the growth of interlocking systems was such as to reward outstanding unscrupulousness and outstanding managerial skill alike. Nor was it only investors who suffered from highly unscrupulous management techniques. For many years safety standards were appallingly low, with accidents commonly caused by defective track.

Freight rates were an area of competition which had more widespread consequences. The essence of rate competition lay in the two types of costs incurred by the railroads, namely the fixed costs of maintaining the system and the running cost of conveying a particular load over a particular distance. Over a route where competition existed, it was tempting for a railroad to calculate its rates on the basis of running cost alone, leaving the fixed costs to be met from other sources – such as another route where it enjoyed a monopoly, and where rates would be correspondingly higher.

Other abuses included discriminatory rates charged for different commodities, or for different journeys. In practice this meant that influential customers, such as those who supplied a

large volume of freight, could demand lower rates: it was tempting for the railroads, as long as they could cover their running costs, to comply with such demands, if only to deprive their competitors of the business. But its effect, in leaving the fixed costs to be met from other sources, was to subsidize big customers at the expense of small. And where the railroad had no competition it would be free to charge whatever it thought fit. Again, there was the formation of rate pools, whereby competing railroads, finding the cost of competition ruinous, might agree on uniformly high rates.

The customers who were most susceptible to such practices, and those who were liable to suffer the most, were the farmers, whose products were worthless without transportation, and

in many cases immediate transportation, to the markets. And it was the farmers who were first to organize their resistance to such sharp practices.

In 1867 an organization was founded known as the National Grange, officially the Patrons of Husbandry. It originated as a social and educational institution, but during the 1870s, when nearly a million farmers, predominantly in the Midwest, became members, the National Grange rapidly evolved into a political force, co-ordinating the votes of its members to ensure the election of state legislators sympathetic to their cause, and the consequent enactment of legislation to outlaw the most common abuses.

Union Pacific fruit train, and (inset) itinerant harvest workers in 1890.

The railroads had grown used to controlling political and judicial processes to their own advantage: and the Grangers were encouraged when, at first, the railroads' appeals against the new measures were dismissed by the Supreme Court. However, in 1886 the same court reversed its earlier decision when it ruled that states had no power to regulate rates charged on traffic that passed beyond their own borders, thus undermining the Granger cause, and providing another illustration of the need for federal regulation.

The process of consolidation of individual routes into ever larger systems, which had been the principal cause of the competition that engendered the rate wars and their accompanying evils, was only hastened by the mounting attacks to which the railroads found themselves subject. In fact, the main force behind the co-operation between railroads that gradually replaced much of the competition toward the end of the nineteenth century was the leading banker of the day, J. Pierpont Morgan.

Morgan had become involved in railroads in spectacular fashion during one of the skirmishes in the 'Erie wars' of the late 1860s. After reaching a compromise with Vanderbilt, Gould and Fisk found a new outlet for their acquisitive tendencies in the growing traffic from the coalfields of northern Pennsylvania. A new line from Binghamton to Albany, the Albany and Susquehanna, was about to be opened in 1869, and Gould and Fisk, acting through the agency of the Delaware and Hudson Canal Company, attempted to buy out the A & S. They found themselves opposed by Morgan, in alliance with the Lackawanna and Western Railroad, and after reaching a stalemate the conflict was eventually settled by a trackside battle, in which Morgan's 'army' prevailed, and a bitter legal and political struggle which the Erie men finally abandoned as fruitless.

As his banking interests grew, Morgan found himself increasingly caught up with the railroads. By 1879 he was a director of Vanderbilt's New York Central, and in 1880 he was instru-

mental in raising $40,000,000 for the tottering Northern Pacific. During the 1870s railroad construction, funded by private investors or by the local communities that were enabled by the General Bonding Law of 1869 to raise money to buy railroad securities, had far outstripped demand: many new lines were built without any hope of immediate financial return, and by the end of the 1870s bankruptcies were common. In 1879 alone, 65 railroads with a combined capitalization of well over $200,000,000 were foreclosed. Even those railroads that avoided outright insolvency found themselves paying annual interest charges on existing debts that could amount to half or more of their net earnings.

Nevertheless, each panic, after a few years while the markets recovered, was followed by a new outbreak of uneconomic building. Nowhere were the consequences of this felt more acutely than in New York, which in

Cartoonist's view of Cornelius Vanderbilt and Jim Fisk in 1870.

1880 had nearly 6,000 miles of main line, and where almost 2,000 more were added in the ensuing decade.

The competition was fiercest between the major trunk routes. The New York Central and the Erie, both with extensive networks of feeder lines, were also subject to competition from the Baltimore and Ohio and the Pennsylvania for traffic to the Midwest. In the early 1880s the Pennsylvania, which dominated traffic in its native state, was expanding most rapidly, at the expense of the other three.

The same period saw the appearance of new railroads whose sole purpose seemed to be to duplicate the existing routes and force the incumbents to buy them out. In 1878 Vanderbilt had been forced to buy the new Nickel Plate – the New York, Chicago and St Louis Railway – to protect his Lake Shore route to Chicago, and in 1883 the West Shore Railroad began building up the Hudson in direct competition with the New York Central. William Vanderbilt, believing the Pennsylvania to be behind these encroachments, responded with his own

counterattack, selecting the small but prosperous coal-carrying Philadelphia and Reading Railroad as the basis for a new venture, the South Pennsylvania Railroad.

By 1885 Morgan, whose own reputation as a financier of the railroads was suffering by association with such suicidal competition, concluded that 'something should be done.' His solution was that Vanderbilt and the Pennsylvania should buy each other's competing railroads, Vanderbilt taking over the West Shore and the Penn the South Pennsylvania. Morgan was able to impose this compromise on the reluctant rivals, and in the process took charge of reorganizing the South Pennsylvania, West Shore and Philadelphia and Reading, being named as owner of the South Pennsylvania to circumvent a state ordinance prohibiting the Penn itself from buying competing railroads.

Morgan, like others before him, then found his interests spreading to the west: and, like his predecessors, he found himself in conflict with other powerful and ambitious men. Attempt-

ing to extend the Vanderbilt system into Iowa from Chicago, he was blocked by Edward Harriman, who in 1881 had gained control of the Illinois Central and had guided it through prosperity toward expansion. That first clash in 1886, over the obscure Dubuque and Sioux City Railroad, was won by Harriman: soon they were contesting more substantial spoils.

In 1893 the Erie finally collapsed and Morgan, charged with restructuring the company, again found himself opposed by Harriman, who succeeded in imposing some of his own conditions on the process of reorganization. Two years later another railroad which had suffered in the past from the dead hand of Jay Gould – the Union Pacific – collapsed along with over 150 others. The state of the UP by then was such that not even Morgan was interested in attempting to salvage it, and Harriman, now enjoying the backing of the Standard Oil concern, assumed control. Within five years Harriman transformed the Union Pacific into a booming business, and on the death of

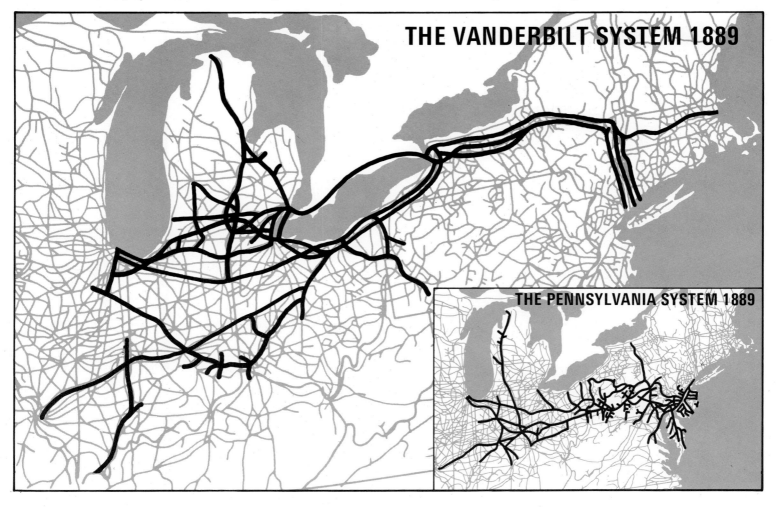

THE VANDERBILT SYSTEM 1889

THE PENNSYLVANIA SYSTEM 1889

Collis Huntington in 1900 he raised $50,000,000 to take control of the Southern Pacific.

Morgan, meanwhile, had formed an alliance with James Hill to establish the common ownership of the Northern Pacific and Great Northern monopoly in the northeast, and had seen the Chicago, Burlington and Quincy added to this system. In New England he extended his control of the New York, New Haven and Hartford Railroad to incorporate many of the smaller operations in the area; and he used his influence in the region to block the planned expansion of the Philadelphia and Reading (which, since its part in the Penn-New York Central standoff, had grown to a 5000-mile system) until he could assume control. In the southeastern states, where the depradations of the Civil War had been followed by spurious constructors appropriating state funds with little attempt to construct the railroads they were intended to finance, Morgan applied his organizational skills to the creation of the 9000-mile Southern Railways system.

He was also able to exercise authority over all the New York trunk routes and their associated feeders, so that coal traffic was evenly distributed and uniform rates were charged.

Nor was this the limit of Morgan's activities, for he was active in every area of major industry, imposing his own brand of order on the financial workings of half the country, epitomized by his part in the formation of the mammoth US Steel trust. But such an empire can only be fueled by its own growth, and the growth of the Morgan railroad empire led inevitably to a final conflict with Harriman.

The area of conflict was the northwest, where the takeover by James Hill, Morgan's ally, of the Chicago, Burlington and Quincy provoked Harriman, who was also seeking a rail entry into Chicago for his Union Pacific-Southern Pacific system, into a fantastic scheme of his own. Refused a share in the Burlington by Hill, he decided to buy control of the Northern Pacific itself in order to obtain its Burlington holdings.

The resulting battle took on epic proportions. As the financial might of Morgan and Hill was ranged against that of Harriman and his ally, Rockefeller, outsiders joined in, but their short selling of the soaring Northern Pacific stock backfired when the price kept rising and there was no more stock to buy. The resulting financial panic could only be ended by a truce between the two factions, and eventually a new holding company was established in which both sides had an interest – the Northern Securities Corporation. In the course of the affair Morgan gave the game away with his reply to a reporter who asked for a statement in the public interest, asserting 'I owe the public nothing.'

Meanwhile, the representatives of the public to whom Morgan felt himself under no obligation had made some efforts to impose their own control. Following the Supreme Court's decision of 1886 that states could only regulate rates within their own boundaries, the Interstate Commerce Act was passed by Congress in February 1888. This Act

By the beginning of the century Edward Harriman was one of the leading railroad operators. At the time the Union Pacific train (below left) was photographed at Genoa, Nebraska, in 1894 the railroad was close to collapse, and the following year Harriman took it over. Under his administration the Union Pacific was transformed into one of the country's most successful railroads, and on the death of Collis Huntington in 1900 he was able to add the Southern Pacific to his other interests. The simultaneous growth of the powerful railroad interests of J. Pierpoint Morgan, in alliance with the northwestern empire of James Hill, represented (below) by a passenger car on the Northern Pacific's North Coast Limited in April 1900 featuring the first electric lights to be used on a northwestern transcontinental train, led to inevitable conflict between the two. The resulting battle for control of the Northern Pacific ended in a national financial panic.

banned pools, discriminatory rates, preferential treatment and the other common abuses, laid down that rates must be 'just and reasonable,' and established the Interstate Commerce Commission to enforce its provisions. But the ICC was virtually devoid of any power to enforce them, and public skepticism was not diminished when 15 of the 16 rate cases in which the Supreme Court adjudicated between the passing of the Act and 1905 went in the railroads' favor.

Governments had been slow to act in other areas of railroad operation too. The standard gauge was not legally established until 1886. The Westinghouse airbrake, which made possible dramatic improvements in efficiency as well as safety, was adopted only slowly; and the universal coupling, another device which was to save the lives of hundreds of railroad brakemen annually, was not made a legal requirement until 1893, when the airbrakes were also made mandatory.

Finally, after the Northern Pacific debacle of 1901 the government was compelled to act. The railroads themselves were ready for legislation by this time, as the years of competition had taken their toll and they were now suffering from the abuses they had imposed on others, with the biggest shippers able to demand covert rebates on the published freight rates. Accordingly, the Elkins Act of 1903 strengthened the Interstate Commerce Act by making any deviation from the

published rates illegal, without any need for customers to take court action to prove their case.

The ICC was further strengthened in 1906 by the Hepburn Act, which extended its powers to cover activities of the railroads other than the purely operational, increased the size of the commission, gave it powers to establish maximum rates and made the commission's decisions binding. In 1916 the eight-hour day was made standard.

In 1917 there was more dramatic government intervention. The increased labor costs brought about by the imposition of the eight-hour day, and rates that the ICC had steadfastly refused to increase, brought the entire system to the brink of collapse as the nation's involvement in the First World War brought record freight movements to the east coast. For just over two years from the end of 1918 the railroads were placed under government control.

Conditions after the First World War, when the railroads were returned to their owners, were to prove very different from the years which had seen their growth. New forms of competition would erode their monopoly of transport, and the quarter of a million miles they reached in 1916 would prove to be a peak from which, slowly and painfully, they would be forced to recede.

The Westinghouse air brake was first fitted to this locomotive of the Pennsylvania in 1869, but was not a legal requirement until 1893.

PRIVATE ENTERPRISE AND PUBLIC SERVICE

By the time the federal government assumed control of the railroads at the end of 1917, the men who had dominated the scene during the years of expansion had gone. Gould, Vanderbilt, Morgan, Jim Hill and Ed Harriman had followed their own visions, looting, empire-building or rationalizing as their tastes dictated, and had left their legacies in the systems they created or destroyed.

Increasing government control in the early years of the new century built on the order that Morgan had sought to impose, as the ICC's powers were extended, but the railroads themselves had welcomed the standardization of rates and had otherwise carried on more or less as they pleased. Traffic, revenue and earnings were more than doubled between 1900 and 1913, but depression in 1913–14 caused a small drop in traffic and a rather larger drop in income: there was still far too much spare capacity and in the two years to 1915 some 15,000 miles of track – about 6 per cent of the total – were in receivership. Too much money had been spent on corporate rearrangement of the kind which saw the Pennsylvania Railroad acquire large holdings in the Baltimore and Ohio and other northeastern systems, at the expense of track and rolling stock maintenance and replacement, so that the large increase in traffic that followed the outbreak of war in Europe found the railroads unable to cope.

The main symptom of this inability was the breakdown of the system whereby freight cars run over 'foreign' roads were returned to their owners. The massive increase in freight traffic to the northeastern ports was more than the operators in the region could handle, and as the backlog of empty cars grew, the unloading of full cars at New York and New Jersey began to be impeded, while a nationwide shortage of cars increased to alarming proportions. The establishment of the Railroad War Board in 1917 had little effect, and ultimately the government was forced to take over.

The government's conduct of the railroads was subsequently the subject of much controversy. Industry propaganda held that efficiency had deteriorated, that the policy of rerouting traffic from the Pennsylvania and the Baltimore and Ohio onto the New York state trunk routes was misguided, and that railroad property was neglected: the Director General of Railroads contended that efficiency was improved by standardization of operation, and that new equipment purchased and compensation paid to the operators amounted to a large government subsidy.

By the beginning of the twentieth century the railroads' provision of facilities for passengers included every modern convenience, such as the vacuum cleaner and telephone exhibited (below) in the observation car of the Oriental Limited. Washing facilities were standard on long-distance journeys, as in the scene on a Santa Fe express (opposite) at the turn of the century, though not all trips can have been quite as jolly as that being enjoyed by the ladies (opposite, below) on the same railroad a few years later.

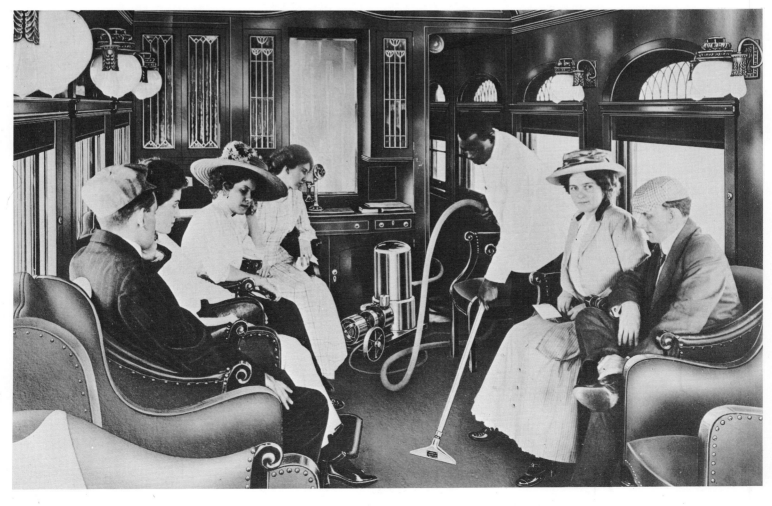

southern prairies dangerously exposed to infiltration by railroads being built in the northwestern states, not to mention the annexation that was being demanded by many American politicians at the time. In any case, Hill seems to have decided in advance that the Bow River route through Kicking Horse Pass should be followed, going so far as to offer the new surveyor, Major A. B. Rogers, a bonus of $5000 for discovering a usable Kicking Horse route. Rogers duly found his route, through the pass that still bears his name, though he sadly underestimated the severity of the grades involved.

Even when luck, politics and commercial considerations had played their part in determining the general direction to be followed, there was still the precise work of measurement to be done. In the case of Fleming's original surveys for the transcontinental line, no fewer than 2000 men were involved, and of the 46,000 miles reconnoitred on foot, a quarter were subject to the detailed measuring and recording process of the instrument survey.

So – reverting to the standard procedure for locating the line – the engineer-in-chief, with the benefit of the data collected by the instrument party, would then be in a position to make the final selection of the route to be followed. At this point, virgin territory might be selected as most likely to provide the easiest possible course; alternatively, the presence of established towns or the location of physical features such as mountain passes or bridging points on rivers might be a deciding factor; or, again, where a specific feature such as a mine in a mountainous area, was the eventual destination, the railroad would have to follow whatever route could be found.

No matter what the circumstances, the choice of route was critical, since a poor track could always be improved, whereas a mistake in location might mean abandoning the line and starting all over again. The main elements to be taken into account were the sharpness of curves and the steepness of grades. Generally speaking, American railroads permitted much sharper curves than their European counterparts, with curves under 300 ft in radius being relatively common, while in Europe

The difficulties of building the first transcontinental railroad were at their greatest in the mountain sections, where keeping the grades within reasonable limits involved a great deal of cutting, filling, tunneling and bridging. Opposite: Tipping earth to form an embankment in Heath's Ravine on the Central Pacific's route through the Sierra Nevada, 1865. Left: Excavating a cutting by stages to the west of Weber Canyon, Utah, nearing the end of the Union Pacific's westward progress in the fall of 1868. Below: Laying tracks on the prepared roadbed of the Prescott and Eastern Railroad through Arizona Territory in 1898.

1000 ft was generally the minimum radius allowed on main lines. This was one of the reasons for the swiveling pilot truck and equalized driving wheels suspension of the American Standard locomotive that was adopted universally in the early years of the railroads. The penalty for increasing the sharpness of curves is inevitably a reduction in permissible speeds.

Gradients allowed less room for maneuver. The low degree of friction between metal rail and metal wheel that make the railroad such an economical form of transport – a 40-ton railcar set rolling at 60 mph on level track will travel for five miles before coming to a stop, five times as far as a motor truck in comparable conditions on a highway – imposes limits on the grades a locomotive can negotiate before its wheels start to slip; and even a slight increase in the grade will cause a dramatic reduction in the weight of train that can be hauled by a locomotive.

On the other hand, building a straight, level track will almost certain-ly involve much more labor in cutting through hills and filling in hollows. Such work was made considerably easier when the first steam shovels were introduced, and the development of sophisticated modern earth-moving equipment steadily expanded the potentialities in comparison with manual operations. But additional cutting and filling, by whatever means, increases the expense of construction, so that the art of railroad location has always been to achieve the best balance between construction costs and eventual operating convenience.

In fact, this basic compromise became a distinctive feature of American railroads during the nineteenth century. The accepted principle was to select the right route, build the road as quickly and economically as possible, bypassing obstacles even at the expense of making a longer or slower line, and then, once the trains were running and the revenue was coming in, use the proceeds to improve the track and carry out such major works as might prove desirable.

One of the best known examples of this process in operation eliminated the historic meeting place of the original Union Pacific and Central Pacific lines at Promontory, in Utah. In 1904 the Southern Pacific, which by then had absorbed the Central Pacific, laid a new line 132 miles long across the Great Salt Lake, not only saving 44 miles in distance over the old route but also avoiding many severe grades and sharp curves. More recently, in 1967, the Southern Pacific eliminated another bottleneck in its operations by means of a new line from Palmdale, California, to the classification yard at Colton. Previously, freight from the northwest bound for the southern sections of the railroad had to pass through Los Angeles on the original San Joaquin Valley line. To eradicate consequent delays, a new line was built from Palmdale through the Cajon Pass to Colton, the whole 78 miles of new main line together with 12 miles of associated sidings being constructed, with the aid of the most modern equipment available, in only fifteen months.

The American Standard locomotive, typified by No 119 (above) and the restored *Jupiter* (opposite) at Promontory was evolved to meet the demands of twisting track. The Promontory section was by-passed in 1904, and in 1967 the Southern Pacific opened its new line through the Cajon Pass in California (right).

Another notable cutoff was constructed on the Denver and Rio Grande Western to shorten the distance between Denver and the west via Salt Lake City. Originally, the route involved a lengthy detour to the south via Pueblo, but the completion of the 6.2-mile Moffat Tunnel between Bond and Dotsero in 1928 enabled the Dotsero cutoff to be brought into operation, reducing the distance by some 65 miles.

A year after the opening of the Moffat Tunnel, the Cascade Tunnel on the Great Northern line through the Cascade mountain range in the state of Washington became the longest in North America. It was actually the second line improvement on this section

Above and right: Construction work on the entrance to the Canadian Pacific's Connaught Tunnel. This tunnel was brought into use in 1916 to eliminate the final stages of the climb to the summit of Rogers Pass, which originally involved 17 miles of grades of over 2%. The Connaught Tunnel, double tracked and five miles long, carries the main line 552 ft below the summit of the pass, and as well as shortening the distance by more than four miles enabled more than six full circles of curvature to be dispensed with, along with the miles of snow sheds that were needed to protect the track from avalanches. The Great Northern Railway's Cascade Tunnel (opposite, top), some 7.8 miles long, is the longest in North America, and replaced an earlier 2.6-mile tunnel. Electric operation of the earlier route was extended with the construction of the new tunnel, completed in 1929, to cover a 71-mile section of the route between Appleyard and Skykomish.

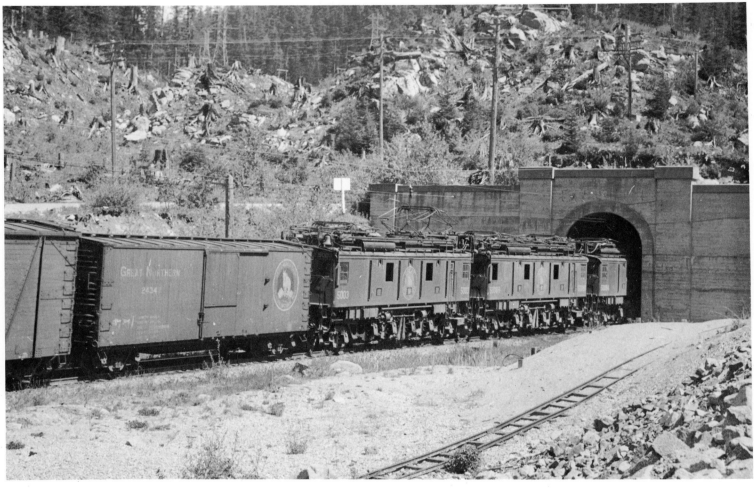

of the Great Northern, a 2.6-mile tunnel having been completed in 1900 to avoid the original switchbacks through the mountains. Heavy approach grades were still needed, however, and with the competition of the Milwaukee Road on the route to Seattle the Great Northern began a further stage of improvement. Not only was the 7.8-mile Cascade Tunnel built, but a 71-mile section of track was electrified, and a 10-mile reduction in the overall distance was accompanied by the elimination of several miles of snowsheds, older tunnels and grades in excess of 2 per cent.

Perhaps the most spectacular of all such improvements, however, are those carried out on the Canadian Pacific main line over Kicking Horse Pass. From the east, seven miles of grades in excess of 4 per cent down into the Columbia valley were followed, after a relatively level stretch, by another spell of 2.2 per cent grades up to Rogers Pass. In steam days this involved using as many as three locomotives to propel a mere eight cars over the passes, and the dangers of the descent going west were matched by the difficulties in working the eastbound trains back up. Avalanches were an additional hazard in winter, and the miles of loops involved in reaching the heights were another drawback.

The first stage in improving this situation was the boring of the famous spiral tunnels under Field Hill. Switchbacks, which extended the principle of the zigzag up a mountainside, whereby grades are made easier at the expense of additional distance by adding loops at the ends of the straight sections, were an early solution to the problem of taking railroads up hills. The Field Hill tunnels virtually extended this practice inside the mountain: one, 3206-ft long, turns through 234 degrees and is followed by another, 2890 ft in length, with a further 232 degrees of turn, and together they produce a drop of 93 ft.

The second stage was the completion of the five-mile Connaught Tunnel in 1916, which eliminated turns amounting to more than six full circles, as well as five miles of snowsheds, and lowered

the summit of the line by 540 ft. Although this left some heavy grades to be worked, the task was made easier with the introduction of diesel power and its facility for multiple operation.

In the 1970s, however, with predictions of a 60 per cent increase in traffic during the 1980s pointing to mounting pressure on the Rogers Pass section, C.P. Rail began planning a new grade improvement. This will involve some 21 miles of new track, incorporating a nine-mile tunnel that will be the longest in North America and which is expected to take four years to complete.

When the railroads were first built, such schemes were rarely considered, and the next steps after deciding on the location were to make working plans, secure rights of way and prepare the project for letting to the many subcontractors who were usually involved. Grading was carried out first, and ideal-

The Connaught Tunnel requires constant ventilation, provided by the fan house at the western entrance (right). Modern track uses continuously welded rails, like those laid on the B & O (below).

ly the cutting and filling were balanced so that material dug away to run the line through rising ground could be used to form the embankments which carried it across depressions. Culverts at the bottom of the embankments would be included to allow the passage of any watercourses. On level ground, to keep the roadbed above the surface so as to improve drainage and minimize interference from drifting snow, ditches dug alongside would provide the material for the raised bed.

Next came the crossties for supporting the rails. In the early days various systems were tried, including piles sunk in the ground and stone sills laid along the surface, but wooden ties quickly came to be the accepted method. As techniques improved, it became customary to treat the wooden ties chemically to prolong their lives, usually with creosote applied under great heat and pressure. A system of steel ties was developed by the Carnegie Steel company, and used for a time on the Bessemer and Lake Erie Railroad early in the twentieth century. In recent years reinforced concrete ties have gained favor, although less than half

of one per cent of the total of over 25,000,000 ties laid annually are of anything except wood.

With the ties in place, it was time to lay the rails. Again, there has been great improvement in the standard of rail employed. At first, iron rails weighing only 30 lb per yard were the standard, but over the years the weight was increased, and from the 1870s rails of rolled steel began to be used. Current practice is to use rails of 132 lb per yard and weights of up to 155 lb have been adopted by some railroads. Whereas the earliest procedure was to use only four spikes per rail, this number was increased to give greater support as the trains grew heavier. Recently, welded rail has come to be recognized as the ideal, the gaps that previously occurred every 13 yards being eradicated to give a smoother ride at high speeds, though its use is generally confined to the busiest main lines.

The actual process of tracklaying has been automated, with impressive results. Machines are used to lift the old rails and remove old ties, insert new ties and pack new ballast around them. Such operations are expensive: in 1977

the Rock Island line was spending $5,000,000 on rehabilitating 134 miles of its double track between Joliet and Rock Island itself, the road having deteriorated badly since the 1950s, when the effects of a general declines in traffic were accentuated by heavy competition on its main lines. The consequence of such deterioration can be even more costly – reductions in permissible speeds and operating efficiency, leading inevitably to further erosion of business.

In the past, before the introduction of such specialized machinery, laying new track necessitated the employment of large numbers of men, though with a high degree of organization some impressive results were achieved. In 1887 the St Paul, Minneapolis and Manitoba system was extended 545 miles through Dakota and Montana between April and October. Some 10,000 men were involved, and a considerable amount of work remained to be done before the road was complete, but while that was being done the line was already earning. Twenty years later, the Milwaukee Road was built for 2300 miles across Montana, Idaho and Washington to Seattle in only three years.

Maintenance of the track, once laid, is of paramount importance. Ideally, the line on busy sections will be inspected twice a day for any misalignment or other fault. One of the main reasons for the Pennsylvania Railroad's pre-eminence towards the end of the last century was its comprehensive program of track maintenance, which was reinforced by annual inspections of the whole road, with prizes awarded to the supervisors and foremen in charge of the best-kept sections.

Whatever the efforts of the locating engineer to keep the track on level ground, building railroads soon involved the building of bridges to carry them across rivers, ravines and valleys which were too deep for embankments to be practical: and as with other aspects of the railroads in America, bridges soon developed distinctive features.

Stone arches, of the type commonly found in Europe, were used where stone was available and a permanent structure desirable. The approaches to the Harlem Valley bridge, for example,

Above: A track gang positions 440-yard sections of rail ready for welding on the Santa Fe main line.

Below: A 780-ft timber trestle built by United States Military Railroad engineers at Whiteside, Tennessee.

Above: A Santa Fe engineer uses a radio to supervise the unloading of the rail sections from flat cars.

Below: The Columbia bridge carrying the Pennsylvania Railroad over the Schuylkill River, in 1859.

were carried on 60-ft granite spans, and the Pennsylvania Railroad's depot in Philadelphia was reached over a series of brick arches, each spanning one street. But the sheer number and size of rivers and other obstacles that had to be crossed, and the high-quality stone and skilled labor that such structures demanded, ruled them out as a normal solution.

The obvious substitute for stone was wood, and the wooden trestle quickly became a standard feature of the North American railroad. The Baltimore and Ohio, in its progress across Maryland, reached Harper's Ferry in 1834, and was held up at this point until the first railroad bridge was opened two years later. A remarkable feature of this bridge was its incorporation of a junction with the branch line to Washington in the middle of the river, though floods which washed away the bridge at regular intervals soon put a stop to the arrangement, and a metal bridge was erected in its place in 1852.

Ideally, weathered timber at least two years old was needed for sound construction, but as the railroads spread out across the west there was a great temptation to use fresh wood, which naturally shrinks and warps with the passage of time. An ingenious solution to this problem was the use of the Howe truss, which featured adjusting screws at the joints to compensate for shrinkage and distortion of the timbers.

The primary advantage of the timber trestle was that it could be erected by unskilled workmen using materials readily available, and for the first few decades of railroad construction it was the standard form of bridge. A great drawback, however, was the need for constant maintenance, with the wooden members needing to be replaced at regular intervals as they rotted, and from the 1870s iron came to be used instead.

Nevertheless, the wooden trestle was a vital part of the railroads' growth, and some of the longest bridges ever built were of this type. Longest of all was the 20-mile trestle across the Great Salt Lake which formed part of the Lucin cutoff on the Southern Pacific's bypassing of the old Promontory route. Completed in 1904, the Salt Lake bridge was gradually replaced by an embankment formed of earth tipped over the sides, and this was the fate of many of the early timber trestles in the west.

More spectacular than the Salt Lake trestle was the Great Trestle on the old Colorado Midland Railway's line in the Rockies. Over 1000 ft long, the Great Trestle formed part of a system of loops by which the Colorado Midland reached the Ivanhoe Pass, and carried the road on a curve. This structure was abandoned in 1900 after snow had rendered the line unusable for several weeks.

A related type of timber construction found commonly on mountain railroads were the snowsheds built to protect the line from blockage by drifting snow and destruction by avalanches. The scale of the problem is indicated by the amounts of snow involved, up to 250,000 cubic yards weighing over 100,000 tons often being encountered in a single slide. Canadian Pacific engineers even calculated that the air currents set up by the mountains of sliding snow could split a 2-ft tree trunk. Consequently, snowsheds were a vital part of railroad

building, and the Central Pacific, which encountered such severe weather in its passage across the Sierra Nevada, at one time had 60 miles of sheds protecting its road.

When wood came to be replaced generally by metal in the 1870s, an unintentional spur to the builders' ingenuity was provided by the perpetuation of the old system of contracting for construction by the foot. Given the relative prices of the materials involved, the contractors were forced to devise construction methods that used the least possible amount of iron.

The basic element of most bridges was the truss, which is effectively a girder incorporating a framework of in-

Four diesels head a unit tanker train over the Canadian Pacific's Lethbridge viaduct, which carries the line at a height of 314 ft over the Old-man River, Alberta. In the Canadian mountain sections avalanches were a major hazard, and miles of snow sheds were needed to protect the track (bottom).

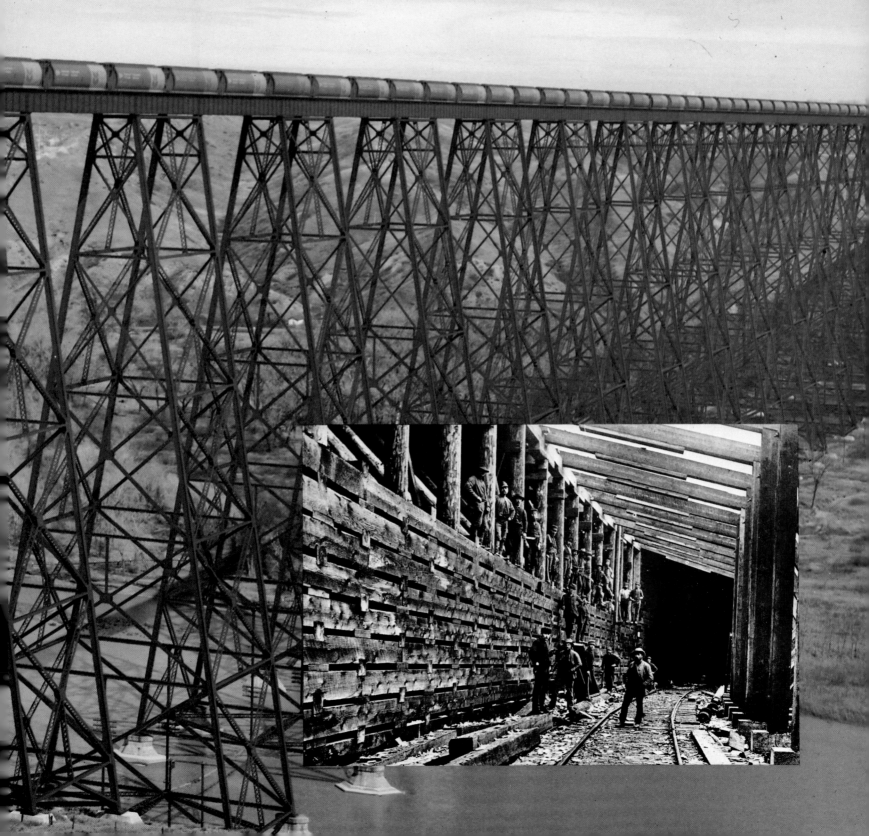

dividual members. At first, trusses were built up of plates in the form of a box, and this method was used by the English engineer Robert Stephenson for his famous Victoria bridge over the St Lawrence at Montreal. The undoubted strength of such structures was only obtained at the expense of constant maintenance – the Victoria bridge included no less than 30 acres of metal which had to be painted at regular intervals – and a telling comment on the more pragmatic construction methods used by North American engineers was provided by Stephenson himself, in his reported comment to the architect of the Niagara suspension bridge, 'If your bridge succeeds, mine is a magnificent blunder.' Completed in 1855, the Niagara Falls bridge did succeed, and the plate form of construction was never used widely in North America. In general, however, the flexibility of suspension bridges, overcome in the Niagara model by forming the span of two floors trussed together, has prevented their widespread adoption for railroad use.

The need for economy in construction of iron bridges encouraged the use of metal pins in preformed holes rather than rivets for connecting the members, which, as mentioned, were kept to the minimum. Where very wide rivers had to be crossed, a series of trusses would be supported on masonry or metal-framed piers. The foundations for the piers in a river might be built by the use of a coffer dam, from which the water could be pumped, or by sinking wooden piles in the river bed.

Often the piers would have as much of their height under the water as above the surface. In the case of the bridge over the Ohio river at Cairo, built by the Illinois Central in the late 1890s, the engineers had to allow for a difference between high- and low-water marks of as much as 60 ft, while the St Louis bridge over the Mississippi had piers whose underwater depth was twice the height of the superstructure above the water.

Where piers are not used for support, increasing the length of the span means a corresponding increase in the depth of the truss. The longest single girder is found on the Burlington Northern's Metropolis bridge over the Ohio at

128

Paducah, Kentucky. The span of 720 ft requires a truss 110 ft deep. Conversely, as long as piers can be provided, there is practically no limit to the number of consecutive girders which can be linked to form the bridge, as exemplified by the Southern Pacific's Huey P. Long bridge which crosses the Mississippi at New Orleans, the 4.4-mile total length including a longest single span of 790 ft.

When the provision of supports for the bridge becomes impossible, one solution is the cantilever system, which uses self-supporting structures built out from the ends to support a smaller girder in the center. Cantilevers are used for the biggest river crossings, and the longest-span railroad bridge of all, the Canadian National's Quebec bridge over the St Lawrence, is a cantilever. The Quebec bridge had an unfortunate start in life, with a design fault leading to the collapse of one of the incomplete cantilevers in 1907, and after work was resumed in 1910 the central span was dropped in the river during the first attempt to raise it into position in 1916. The span was finally fixed in place in 1917.

Other cantilever bridges have been built in Canada, including the Lachine bridge over the St Lawrence at Montreal and the Niagara cantilever; but the first bridge of this type in North America was built over the Kentucky River at Cincinnati, where a canyon 1200 ft wide and 275 ft deep was regularly subject to surges of 55 ft in the river. Two 177-ft iron piers were built on masonry foundations in the river itself, and three sets of cantilevers were used to bridge the gaps, each span being 375 ft long and carried 276 ft above the river bed.

Finally, the availability of steel, and more recently the use of concrete, has allowed arched bridges to be built without the use of brick or stone. An early example of this type was the St Louis bridge over the Mississippi, where quicksand in the river bed and icefloes and debris in the river itself precluded the use of intermediate piers.

The Santa Fe's bridge over the Mississippi at Fort Madison, Iowa, incorporates a lifting span of 525 ft in its 3347 ft overall length to allow ships to pass.

129

STEAM LOCOMOTIVES

By the middle of the nineteenth century, the American Standard type of locomotive had assumed a form that was to remain in almost universal use for another fifty years. The 4–4–0 wheel arrangement was, of course, first adopted at an early stage, but it was in the early 1850s that Thomas Rogers of the Paterson, New Jersey, firm of Rogers, Ketchum and Grosvenor began to produce the engines that embodied the typical form that was to be so widely imitated.

The most distinctive feature of the

Rogers design was the lengthened wheelbase which allowed the cylinders to be mounted in a horizontal position at the sides of the smokebox, this being carried on the four-wheel pilot truck that had proved so vital in enabling locomotives to cope with the irregularities of early track. The equalizing beams carrying the driving wheels were also a standard feature by this stage, and other characteristics of the Rogers locomotive and its imitators was the tapered boiler surrounding the large firebox at the rear.

Other external features of American locomotives derived directly from their operating environment. Large cabs for engineer and fireman were essential for their protection in the extremes of climate that were encountered; big chimneys with spark-arresters were used to prevent fires in the woods and prairies through which they passed; bells, headlights and cow-catchers were necessary to protect the train and to warn against interlopers on the track; and the big sandbox on top of the boiler enabled the engineer to cope with slip-

ping wheels on remote stretches of line where no assistance could be expected.

Another external characteristic which, however, had no practical reason behind it, was the elaborate ornamentation widely displayed during this period. Bright colors, burnished copper and brass trim, even flags and pictures painted on side panels, were often sported by the early locomotives. The practice died out partly as a result of the ending of the system whereby each crew was allotted its own engine and held responsible for its appearance as well as its mechanical order.

Internally, the American 4–4–0, like all steam locomotives, was based on the principles developed by George Stephenson and embodied in his famous *Rocket* in 1829. The hot gases from a firebox were carried through a system of tubes inside a boiler to a smokebox; the water heated by the tubes formed steam, which was collected and fed into cylinders where, acting on a piston, it drove the wheels by means of a connecting rod. The motion of the wheels was in turn transmitted to the valves admit- ting the steam to the cylinders, allowing the spent steam to escape from the cylinder. The exhaust steam was then fed into the smokebox to create the draft on the fire and so keep the whole process repeating itself.

Wood-burning American 4–4–0s at the United States Military Railroad depot at City Point, Virginia, in 1864. The Baldwin 4–4–0 (inset), built for the Wilmington and Weldon Railroad in 1859, displays typically lavish ornamentation.

During the 1850s and 1860s the 4–4–0 was generally used to haul both passenger and freight trains, neither of which attained any great speeds, but during the 1870s the appearance of the Wootten firebox began to produce changes. The Wootten was designed to burn the powdery residue from anthracite coal that otherwise had been wasted, and its wide, shallow form demanded some reconsideration of the wheel arrangement.

One method tried was known as the camelback or Mother Hubbard: to avoid an excessively long wheelbase, the engineer's cab was built on top of the boiler, leaving the stoker to feed the firebox from a platform on the front of the tender. The cab on top of the boiler had earlier been used by Ross Winans

of Baltimore, and in a series of locomotives for the Baltimore and Ohio Railroad, but then it had been adopted for the purpose of giving the engineer a better view forward. Combined with the Wootten firebox, the camelback arrangement was used by a number of railroads and in several different wheel configurations.

Wootten himself was general manager of the Philadelphia and Reading Railroad at the time, so it was natural that the Reading should be among the principal users of the type. It was originally applied to 4–6–0 freight engines with small driving wheels, but for the Atlantic City route, where the Reading was in direct competition with the Pennsylvania Railroad, Wootten developed a 2–4–2 fast passenger

The reconstructed Union Pacific locomotive *Jupiter*, a product of the Rogers factory.

engine, with the two small trailing wheels supporting the firebox. As well as his own design of firebox, Wootten incorporated another innovation that was the work of Samuel Vauclain of the Baldwin locomotive works.

Vauclain's system of compound working was one of a variety of methods for using the partially expanded steam from one cylinder to work another cylinder, usually of greater diameter to allow for the lower pressure of steam. The distinctive feature of Vauclain's system was that both cylinders drove the same crosshead, thus removing some of the complications.

Baltimore and Ohio locomotives of the Ross Winans 'camelback' type at Martinsburg, Virginia, in 1858.

The Reading 2–4–2s proved rather unstable at the high speeds for which they were designed, and in 1896 Wootten produced a much more significant design using the 4–4–2 wheel arrangement that has become known from its origins as the Atlantic type. The new engines proved capable of covering the 55½ miles between Camden and Atlantic City in a flat 60 minutes, and in special circumstances of turning in an overall speed of 71.6 mph.

The Pennsylvania also adopted the type for its competing services. The Pennsylvania Atlantics reached their highest development in the guise of the

E6 class, first built in 1910, which included another refinement in the form of superheating. This was an invention of a German engineer, Wilhelm Schmidt, and involved collecting the steam in the normal way, then leading it through elements inside the firetubes so that it was superheated to much greater temperatures and pressures before being admitted to the cylinders. With the addition of superheating in 1910, the E6 Atlantics developed 2400 hp, which for their weight of 110 tons made them among the most powerful locomotives ever built. They remained in use until after the Second World War.

The Pennsylvania Atlantics did not use Wootten fireboxes, having adopted the square-topped Belpaire type for the

bituminous coal to which it had easier access than the Reading. The latter persevered with the Wootten, however, and in 1915 added a four-wheel trailing truck to produce a 4–4–4 type. Apart from some high-speed machines built for special services with lightweight trains during the 1930s, this was the last development of the four-coupled passenger engine, the four-wheel trailing truck reaching its true potential in other applications. For mainline passenger service the next type of major importance was the 4–6–2 Pacific.

A slightly earlier type, the 2–6–2 Prairie, had, like the 2–4–2 that preceded the Atlantic, proved unstable at high speeds, though the examples built during the 1900s were among the biggest passenger engines in the world

The 4–4–2 Atlantic was a popular type of passenger locomotive. The two examples shown opposite are a Canadian Pacific Vauclain compound (top), a design dating from 1899, and the Erie Railroad's No 537 near Rutherford, New Jersey, in 1929. The Pennsylvania Railroad K4 Pacific carries test equipment on the smokebox, while the later New York Central 4–6–4 Hudson (below) featured a streamlined casing.

at the time. The first Pacifics were built for the Missouri Pacific Railroad in 1902, thus providing the derivation of their generic name. Again, it was the Pennsylvania which produced the most impressive examples of this engine type, and again the new wheel configuration was combined with other innovations to reach its highest peak of development.

The Pennsylvania's first Pacifics were the K2 class of 1907, and these used the conventional arrangement of cylinders outside the wheels of the leading truck, controlled by a Stephenson-type link motion carried between the wheels. These were replaced by another type of link motion, named after its Belgian inventor, Egide Walschaert, which operated outside the wheels and used more rugged piston valves. By 1914 the original K2 had been developed into the K4 with the addition of the Walschaerts gear. Although only 15 per cent heavier than their predecessors, the K4s developed 33 per cent more tractive effort, and were particularly useful on the Pennsylvania's heavily graded line between New York and Chicago. The

addition of mechanical stokers in the 1920s allowed them to indulge to the full their appetite for fuel, which the stokers had labored hard to satisfy, and as the weight of trains increased they were provided with tenders carrying 24,400 gallons of water and 25 tons of fuel.

On the New York-Chicago run the Pennsylvania's great rival, the New York Central, had a longer but rather easier route, running alongside the Hudson river and Erie Canal to the shores of the Great Lakes, rather than following the Pennsylvania on the direct route across the mountains. The N.Y.C. had also developed a series of Pacifics, starting with the first models in 1905, to take advantage of the easier route by running heavier trains. A series of N.Y.C. Pacifics culminated in the K5 class of 1925, and an indication of the work required from them is given by the 15,000 gallons of water they carried in their tenders.

However, the K5 class were fast approaching the limits of the Pacific's capacity, and the demand for yet heavier locomotives was met in 1927 with the introduction of the first 4–6–4, known as the Hudson, from the location of the Central's main line out of New York. The four-wheel trailing truck was adopted to allow a bigger grate to be used, and a development of the Walschaerts valve gear, the Baker, was used on later models. Another feature of the Hudsons, which had earlier been fitted to the New York Central Pacifics, was the inclusion of a small booster engine on the trailing truck to give extra power when starting.

The original J1 class Hudsons were developed over the years, their ultimate form being reached in the streamlined J3s which achieved fame hauling the prestige Twentieth Century Limited between New York and Chicago in the late 1930s. But the New York Central had a requirement for still greater power, and this was supplied in the form of the 4–8–4 Niagara type, developed from a series of 4–8–2 freight engines, the Mohawks, by way of the L3 class 4–8–2s which had proved capable of speeds in excess of 80 mph even with the relatively small wheels commonly used on freight machines.

Of course, the above account ignores

the many hundreds of different types of passenger engines used by other railroads. The Milwaukee, for example, had followed a similar progression, starting with a series of 4–6–0 types in the 1890s. Both these and the succeeding Atlantic designs employed the Vauclain compound system, and in 1907 another type of Atlantic was produced with the balanced system of compounding. The latter also used two high-pressure and two low-pressure cylinders, but instead of having them in pairs one above the other outside the leading truck wheels, the balanced system mounted the low-pressure pair inside the frames. From this position they drove the axle of the leading pair of driving wheels, which was cranked for the purpose, while the high-pressure cylinders drove the leading coupled wheels in the normal way.

Because of the additional complication, this system was never very popular on American railroads, and the more common Vauclain type was used again on the Milwaukee's last Atlantics in 1908. In 1910 the first class of Pacif-

ics, the F3s, were introduced, to be followed by the F4 class in the next two years, and then the superheated F5 class: ultimately all 160 engines of the three classes were fitted with superheaters.

The Milwaukee, after the completion of its route to Tacoma and Seattle, had to cater for the contrasting demands of this long transcontinental route which, even with its electrified sections, was subject to severe weather, as well as such shorter but more competitive routes as those to Milwaukee, St Paul and Omaha. Until the late 1920s the Pacifics covered both types, but in 1929 a new class of locomotive was introduced in the form of the 4–6–4. The new engines proved exceptionally fast, and on the 86-mile Chicago-Milwaukee route in July 1934 a special high-speed run produced the remarkable speeds of 92.3 mph average over a 65.6-mile section, with a maximum of 103.5 mph.

For the long hauls on the Pacific route, a more powerful type, the S1 4–8–4s, was introduced, the first of

Derelict streamlined Hudson built for the Milwaukee Road.

which was produced by Baldwin in 1930. With a tractive force of over 62,000 lb, compared with the 45,820 lb of the F6 class 4–6–4s, the S1s were capable of hauling the heaviest passenger trains.

During the 1930s the Milwaukee introduced their celebrated streamlined Hiawatha services, and for the Chicago-Minneapolis run, with a train of six cars, the American Locomotive Company (Alco) produced the A class 4–4–2 design in 1935. These proved capable of sustaining speeds of well over 100 mph, but as the popularity of the trains caused their size to be increased to nine and then 12 cars, the F7 4–6–4s, first built in 1938, replaced them. The new engines were able to take the heavier trains at maximum speeds of over 120 mph, and worked one of the fastest-ever steam-hauled scheduled runs in the world, the 81-mph Sparta-Portage section of the Minneapolis-Milwaukee route.

New York Central 4–8–4 Niagara at Albany, New York, in April 1952.

Elsewhere, among the outstanding engines of the late 1930s were the Santa Fe's 3771 class 4–8–4s, which handled the services over the 1791 miles between Kansas City and Los Angeles. Not only were these locomotives capable of completing the through journey in 26 hours, but after only a few hours they would be ready to make the return trip.

By this stage, the need for minimum servicing and maintenance was becoming paramount, as the locomotives had been developed to a peak of speed and power where track limitation rather than locomotive ability was the governing factor in the schedules. It was against the background of increasing competition from new diesel locomotives, one of whose attractions was their greater availability, that the New York Central produced its ultimate development of the Niagara type.

The aim in designing the Niagaras was a 6000-hp engine with a weight to horsepower ratio no higher than that of the 4–6–4s. In pursuit of this end, a new design of boiler was adopted which omitted the steam dome to allow increased diameter; at the same time the firebox, steam passages and superheater elements were made bigger, carbon steel was employed where appropriate, and roller bearings were adopted. Furthermore, to permit a full evaluation of the design, driving wheels of two diameters, 75 in and 79 in, were supplied.

After their appearance in 1945 the S1 Niagaras were employed on the New York-Chicago run, regularly working through the 930 miles from Harmon, where they took over from the electric locomotives that brought the trains out of Grand Central Station, to Chicago. Detailed studies of their performance, compared with that of a group of diesels, were carried out, and it was found that the six Niagaras attained an availability rate of nearly 76 per cent and a utilization rate of over 69 per cent. This amounted to a yearly average milage of 260,000 miles, while the equivalent figure for the diesels, which cost more than twice as much, was 330,000 miles.

Unfortunately, the carbon-silicon steel used for the boiler shells as a weight-saving measure began to develop cracks; faced with the cost of providing new boilers, the management inevitably turned to diesels for their subsequent motive power requirements. Within a few years the same course was followed by every other railroad, although there were various attempts to prolong the use of steam.

While passenger engines were being developed to their ultimate peak, parallel evolution of their freight counterparts was occurring. As early as 1842 Matthew Baldwin had designed a specialized 0–8–0 freight locomotive for the Georgia Central Railway, and while the mechanical complications of this design prevented its adoption by more than a few railroads, larger numbers of smaller wheels were the obvious answer to the freight requirement of increased power at low speeds.

One railroad which had a particular need for increased power was the

Central Pacific, with its steep climb from Sacramento up into the Sierra Nevada, and in 1882 A. J. Stevens produced a successful 4–8–0 design, 20 of which were built for the line. The following year he extended the idea to produce the 4–10–0 *El Gobernador*, but this 65-ton monster proved too much for the track at that time, and had to remain content with being the biggest locomotive in the world rather than a working engine.

In the later stages of the nineteenth century, 2–6–0 Mogul and 2–8–0 Consolidation engines became the standard types for freight operations, with the latter proving more popular. Among the most powerful at the turn of the century were a pair of 2–8–0s built for the iron ore-carrying Bessemer and Lake Erie Railroad by the Pittsburgh Locomotive Works in 1900. Weighing over 250,000 lb and developing a tractive effort of nearly 64,000 lb, these engines were built specially for working the steeply graded line between the railroad's docks at Conneaut and its yard at Albion: other 2–8–0s from the same builder for service on easier parts of the route weighed a more modest 179,000 lb and were capable of a tractive effort of 38,400 lb.

The principal advantage of the eight-coupled layout was to concentrate weight on the driving wheels and as a result improve adhesion. An indication of the popularity of the type in the early years of the twentieth century was the government's orders, totalling 680, for locomotives of the 2–8–0 wheel arrangement for military service in France during the First World War. By early 1918 no fewer than 30 were being completed every day, though by then bigger types were being adopted for regular use.

Since freight locomotives were not called on to match the high speeds required in passenger service, two-wheel leading trucks were normally used, although the Pennsylvania Railroad, for example, produced the first of a long series of 4–8–2s for fast freight duties in 1918. Culmination of the series was the M1a class of 1930, which weighed 342 tons, including the tender, and produced a tractive effort of 64,550 lb.

The more common freight equivalent

of the Pacific passenger engine was the 2–8–2, or Mikado, and while the 9500 or so engines built amounted to less than half the total of nearly 22,000 2–8–0s, no other type came close in terms of numbers. The Santa Fe went one better in 1903 with the production of the first 2–10–2, which used the trailing truck to give greater flexibility on the Santa Fe's mountain divisions, with their heavy grades and sharp curves.

A natural progression from the two-wheel trailing truck was to four wheels at the back supporting a firebox of increased size, and in the mid-1920s both eight-coupled and ten-coupled freight engines appeared with this arrangement. The 2–10–4 was known in the United States as the Texas type, the first being built for the Texas and Pacific Railroad in 1925, while in Canada their use in the mountain regions of the west from 1929 led to their being called

140

Selkirks. Use of the 2–8–4 was pioneered by the New York Central, again in 1925, which gave rise to their common name of Berkshire, after the mountains of western Massachusetts.

Among the biggest of non-articulated freight locomotives were the 4–10–2 and 4–12–2 types built by Alco for the Union Pacific from 1926. The four-wheel pilot trucks allowed the use of three cylinders, thus maximizing the power that could be obtained without

resorting to articulation. Weighing 350 tons, the 90 4–12–2s which were built delivered a tractive effort of 96,600 lb and were capable of working 3800-ton trains at average speeds of 35 mph.

The biggest steam locomotives of all, however, were of the articulated type. The system of articulation used on American railroads was first developed by Anatole Mallet in France toward the end of the nineteenth century, and involved the use of a single boiler to sup-

A Santa Fe 3800 class 2–10–4, one of a long series of ten-coupled express freight engines used by the railroad. The Baltimore and Ohio started a new trend with its 0–6–6–0 Mallet compound No 2400 of 1904 (inset).

ply two sets of cylinders. The steam was used first by a pair of high-pressure cylinders and then fed to a low-pressure pair, but the distinguishing feature of the Mallet system as against other com-

pound systems was the use of two sets of driving wheels on separate chassis, the leading chassis being arranged so that it could turn and swivel and thus negotiate curves satisfactorily.

The first Mallet built in North America was delivered by Alco to the Baltimore and Ohio Railroad in 1904, and within a few years Mallets were very popular for heavy freight duties. As the number of driving wheels was increased from 12 to 16 and even 20, leading and trailing trucks were added to improve riding qualities and later to support an enlarged firebox. The most popular configuration was the 2–6–6–2, while the biggest of the Mallets were the Union Pacific's 4–8–8–4 Big Boys of 1941. The latter were the biggest steam locomotives ever built, weighing 354 tons. Although not the most powerful of all locomotives, the Big Boys were built for speed and efficiency and, like their predecessors on the Union Pacific, the 4–6–6–4 Challengers, were capable of hauling express freight trains at speeds of up to 80 mph.

The Big Boys came into their own on the Union Pacific's route through the mountains between Ogden and Cheyenne, running fruit trains between Ogden and Green river, where the Challengers took over. Both these Union Pacific types, like later Mallets on other U.S. railroads, dispensed with the compound arrangement when the low-pressure cylinders grew so big that they could no longer be accommodated, and the valves were no longer adequate to deal with the volume of steam.

Among the many varieties of Mallet were some unusual designs. In 1914 the Erie took delivery of a 2–8–8–8–2 Triplex Mallet, a type developed by the Baldwin concern which mounted a second set of low-pressure cylinders on the tender, for use as a helper. Although the Erie subsequently bought another two engines of this type, the addition of extra cylinders without extra steam-generating capacity prevented the triplex from becoming a success, while a 2–8–8–8–4 with a larger boiler and slightly smaller cylinders, built for the Virginian Railroad, suffered from the

Among the last steam locomotives built for service on American main lines were the Norfolk and Western J class 4–8–4s (above). The Union Pacific was noted for the size of its locomotives: the 4–8–4 (opposite, top) preserved at Cheyenne, and the 4–6–6–4 at North Platte, Nebraska (opposite) date from the late 1930s.

same deficiencies in steaming. No more successful were the Santa Fe's 2–10–10–2s, which were rebuilds of earlier machines and featured jointed boilers. The Virginian, on the other hand, after its disappointment with the triplex type, bought ten 2–10–10–2 Mallets which proved eminently suitable for their job of helping 6000-ton coal trains up an 11-mile section of 2 per cent grades in the Alleghenies.

Another notable user of Mallets was the Denver and Rio Grande Western on its difficult main lines in the Rockies, while the Southern Pacific developed a cab-first design for its mountain section in the Sierra Nevada between California and Nevada. The use of oil for fuel

142

enabled these 4–8–8–2s, of which 195 were built between 1928 and 1944, to run backwards, in effect, with the tender trailing and the engineer thus provided with the best possible view forward.

As well as being the biggest steam locomotives built in North America, engines of the Mallet type were also among the last. After the Second World War, when American railroads were turning in increasing numbers toward diesel power, the Norfolk and Western Railway, whose main operation was the transport of coal from the mining areas of Kentucky and West Virginia, made a determined effort to improve its locomotives to the point where they could compete, in terms of operating efficiency and availability, with the new diesels.

In its own design offices and its own

locomotive works at Roanoke, the Norfolk and Western produced three new models. The J class 4–8–4, first built in 1941, was designed to haul the prestige passenger services at 100 mph and more, while the A class 2–6–6–4 and Y class 2–8–8–2 articulated types, dating from 1936 and 1948 respectively, were used for freight work, the A class at speeds up to 70 mph and the Y6 class developing maximum power at lower speeds. The real advance with these and the Y6b type, the ultimate development of the Mallet, was the rationalizing of maintenance facilities to the point where less than an hour was required for a complete inspection, refueling and lubrication between runs. Moreover, the Y6b enabled maintenance costs to be reduced by an impressive 37 per cent compared with their predecessors of the Y5 class.

However, even the Norfolk and Western was forced to give way to the advance of the diesel, and although the Y6b remained in production until as late as 1952, by 1957 the N. & W. had placed orders for 75 diesels. Its last steam locomotive, and the last for any mainline railroad in the United States, was an 0–8–0 switcher produced in 1953; but the problems of keeping a steam fleet going when everyone else had turned to diesels finally forced the Norfolk and Western to end steam services in 1960, the last run being made by a Y6b on April 4.

Of course, there were many other varieties of steam locomotive apart from the mainline freight and passenger machines. Some were actually attempts to extend the life of steam, such as the steam turbines with which a few railroads experimented around the

The 90 4–12–2s built by Alco for UP in the late 1920s (opposite) were the longest non-articulated locomotives ever built. Above: A N&W Y6b class 2–8–8–2 is assembled in the Roanoke yard in 1949.

time of the Second World War.

One line of turbine development was represented by the Pennsylvania Railroad's geared turbine 6–8–6 of 1944, which actually saw service but was too far outside the mainstream of development to have a lasting impact. Turbines were also used to generate electricity to power motors on the driving axles, and turbo-electric engines that were built included examples for the Union Pacific in 1938, the Chesapeake and Ohio in 1947 and the Norfolk and Western in 1952; but the interruption of the Second

World War prevented Union Pacific from taking the experiment any further, while the later types simply appeared too late to make any great difference.

An earlier design of locomotive which used geared transmission was designed for the specific purpose of operating on the makeshift railroads built in logging country. This was the Shay, named after the engineer who built the first example in 1880. Engines of this type remained in production until 1945, and actually formed the foundations of the Lima Locomotive Works' rise to its position as one of the main locomotive builders in the United States, along with Baldwin and the American Locomotive Company (Alco).

Another type of logging engine, the chain-drive Robb, was developed in Canada, built in 1903 to run on timber

tracks and featuring a tilted boiler; and other transmission systems were used on the Hieslerand Climax logging types. The former had a V arrangement of the cylinders and was driven by a central shaft and universal couplings; the latter employed a combination of chains and gears.

Apart from such specialized forms of locomotive, there were legions of little 0–6–0 and 0–8–0 switching engines used for making up trains in the classification yards. Often these would be machines past their prime which had been relegated to the yards from the main lines, but many were purpose built for the bigger railroads. It was also in the yards that the earliest forerunners of the new form of motive power that was to displace the fascinating variety of steam made their appearance.

DIESEL AND ELECTRIC POWER

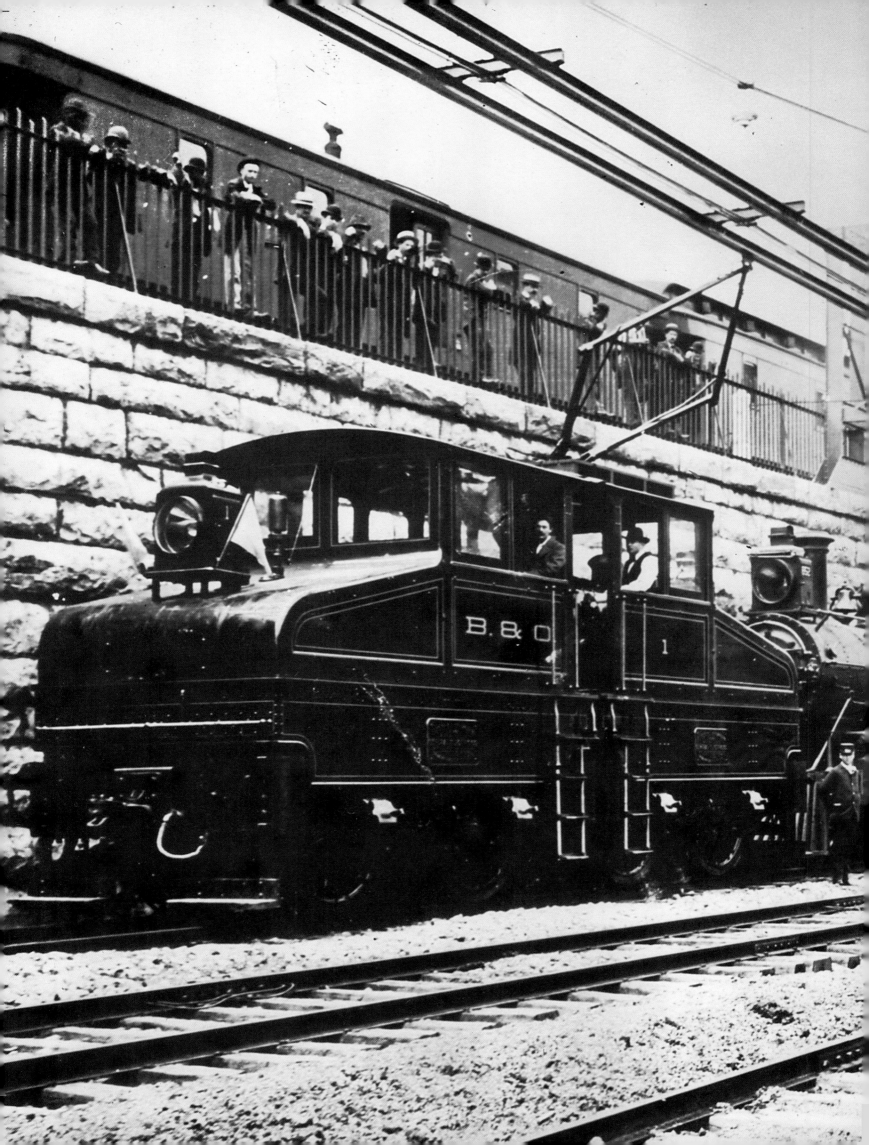

Despite a variety of undoubted advantages over any other method of operation, there was never any real likelihood of electric traction replacing steam on American railroads. The operational benefits can only be realized once the power supply has been provided, and at the time when many main lines in Europe were being electrified, early in the present century, the U.S. network was still growing toward its final total of a quarter of a million miles. The cost of equipping even a fraction of the total with the necessary power supply could not be contemplated when the cost of building the railroads themselves had driven so many companies out of business.

On the other hand, the quietness and absence of pollution associated with electric power made it very attractive in some applications, while the electric locomotive's ability to increase its power output to well over its nominal rating for short periods have enabled trains to be operated in some places where expense or other types of problem might well have made the venture either practically or economically impossible. Its third common application has been in areas where the volume of traffic has been great enough – or the cost of electricity low enough – to make the savings in operating expenses outweigh the initial high equipment expenses, or where automated operation has been desirable on cost or other grounds.

A number of scientists and engineers during the nineteenth century conducted experiments aimed at using electricity to propel a vehicle. As early as the 1880s an electrified tramline was built in Toronto, but the first mainline electrification was carried out in Baltimore in 1895 after the Baltimore and Ohio Railroad was ordered by the city authorities to stop using steam locomotives inside the city. A seven-mile section of track, including the mile-long tunnel under the Patapsco, was fitted with an overhead supply system for 650-volt DC current to enable 1080-hp locomotives to haul trains to the city center.

Early electric operation on the Baltimore and Ohio, the first mainline electrification in the USA.

149

The use of electric traction in North America was restricted generally to routes where steam operation was either difficult or inconvenient. The former category included several mountain areas in the northwestern United States, where both the Great Northern and Milwaukee railroads had substantial electrified sections. The GN's 41-mile scheme (left and opposite) was brought into operation in 1929, and used 11,000-volt alternating current to power Baldwin-Westinghouse locomotives. City centres were also prime candidates for electrification: steam locomotives were banned from Manhattan Island at an early stage, and the Pennsylvania Railroad's construction of its New York terminal, carried out between 1903 and 1910 (below) was accompanied by electrified tunnels under the North and East Rivers. Ultimately the Pennsylvania extended electrification north to New Haven, east to Harrisburg and south to Washington DC, the NY-Washington route being operated by 4260-hp GG-1 locomotives (opposite, below).

New York was another city which acted early to eliminate steam traction from its central districts. Steam locomotives were banned from Manhattan Island after 1908, and by that time the New York Central had electrified its approaches to Grand Central Station from Harmon, some 20 miles away, while the New York, New Haven and Hartford line, first to Stamford, Connecticut, and then to New Haven, was converted by 1907.

The most ambitious electrification scheme in the New York area was carried out by the Pennsylvania Railroad following its acquisition of the Long Island Railroad in 1900. The Long Island line itself was electrified in 1905, and the Pennsylvania's system of tunnels, by which it established its new terminus at Pennsylvania Station, included a through connection with the Long Island system.

The Pennsylvania extended its electrification scheme to the Philadelphia suburban lines from 1915, and by 1933 electric trains were running between Philadelphia and New York. Further work brought the electric service to Washington in 1935, completing a system that included 364 route miles and a total of 1405 miles of track.

Tunnels were other obvious candidates for electrification. The St Clair River Tunnel between Port Huron and Sarnia on the Grand Trunk Railway of Canada's cross-border operation into Michigan was equipped with electric traction in 1908, and the following year the Great Northern's Cascade Tunnel and its approaches followed suit. The Boston and Maine's Hoosac Tunnel was electrified in 1911, and the Mount Royal Tunnel to the Canadian National station in the center of Montreal was operated by electric locomotives as soon as it was completed a few years later.

The 1920s brought further electrification schemes in the new Cascade Tunnel, the 7.8-mile tunnel itself forming part of a system that embraced a total of 72 miles of track, in the Michigan Central's tunnel at Detroit, and on the Illinois Central's suburban lines in Chicago.

Electric locomotives also came into their own on sections of route where steam operation was proving excessively difficult or expensive. The outstand-

ing example was the Milwaukee Road's total of 656 miles of main line in the Rocky and Bitter Root Mountain sections, while the Norfolk and Western and Virginian railroads also used electricity to overcome some severe operating problems.

The Norfolk and Western electrified a 30-mile section between Bluefield and Vivian, where steam locomotives were being pushed to operate the 4000-ton coal trains over 2 per cent grades and through the Elkhorn Tunnel, the initial scheme of 1915 being extended to Williamson in 1926. The line was subsequently rebuilt with easier grades and a new tunnel, and the electric working abandoned. The neighboring Virginian Railroad had similar problems on its route between Mullens and Roanoke, and in the mid-1920s it replaced its big Mallets on this stretch with powerful electric locomotives that could handle coal trains of up to 16,000 tons.

The trouble with such piecemeal development of electrification schemes was that each operator tended to choose its own system, so that research and development suffered; and the long life of electric locomotives further reduced the incentive for any concerted effort at rationalization. One of the results can be seen in the problems experienced by Amtrak in its plans to renew the electrified route between Washington and New York and extend an integrated operation to Boston. The Pennsylvania uses a 12,000-volt 25-cycle AC system on the New York-Washington route, the line to New Haven has been renewed and extended to Boston using 25,000-volt supply, while in New York itself the Metropolitan Transportation Authority lines supply 12,500-volt current at 60 cycles. Without the resources to renew the supply system on the remainder of the New York-Washington sector, Amtrak is faced with the need for locomotives able to operate on all three types of current.

The cost of providing the supply system has also prevented Canadian Pacific from proceeding with a plan to electrify its lines in the mountain regions in the west of the country. The

increased power and traction offered by electric locomotives would solve a lot of Canadian Pacific's problems in the mountains, as well as proving cheaper in terms of fuel cost, but the expense involved would be prohibitive in present economic circumstances.

Some modern industrial lines have been built using electric traction to allow automation. The Carol Lake iron ore mines in northeastern Quebec use a 6-mile track to ferry ore to the crushing plant, while the 15-mile Muskingum Electric Railroad in Ohio and the 78-mile Black Mesa and Lake Powell are other examples, the latter using 6000-hp locomotives to haul 8000-ton coal trains which supply the generating plant on Lake Powell.

However, the appearance of diesel traction has tended to remove the needs that were met originally by some of these electrification schemes. The Milwaukee's electric sections became an inconvenience when diesels proved able to operate satisfactorily over the whole route in the northwest, and a number of other electric operations, such as that

on the Norfolk and Western, were abandoned when the original grades were eased as a result of rebuilding.

In fact, the new form of motive power that completely replaced steam and also eliminated a number of the electric operations effectively overcame the principal drawback to wholesale electrification – the enormous initial cost of installing the power supply system – by combining the flexibility of electric motors with their own generating plant on the same vehicle.

The original Diesel engine was patented by its German inventor in 1892. It was another 20 years before a successful method was found to overcome its main handicap as far as railroad application was concerned, namely how to use the power generated. Various transmission systems have been developed, but the most common, and the universal method on American railroads, was to use the diesel engine to generate electricity, this in turn being utilized to drive axle-mounted electric motors.

In the United States, General

An electrically hauled Great Northern train at Skykomish, on the Cascade electrified section.

Electric produced a 300-hp Bo-Bo – that is, two pairs of axles, each with its own motor – in 1924, and this engine and its derivatives were eventually adopted by many railroads for switching duties. For their power, these early machines were exceptionally heavy: the original 300-hp switcher weighed 60 tons. A similar power-to-weight ratio on a mainline engine would have made it unacceptably massive even if it had been feasible to design such an enlarged version. They were also much more expensive than equivalent steam engines, though this factor was offset by the considerable reduction in fuel costs that they made possible.

Among the many experimental developments of the 1920s and 1930s, one line of research was to prove most significant. This was begun by the Electromotive and Winston Engine companies, which in 1930 became a division of General Motors, and cen-

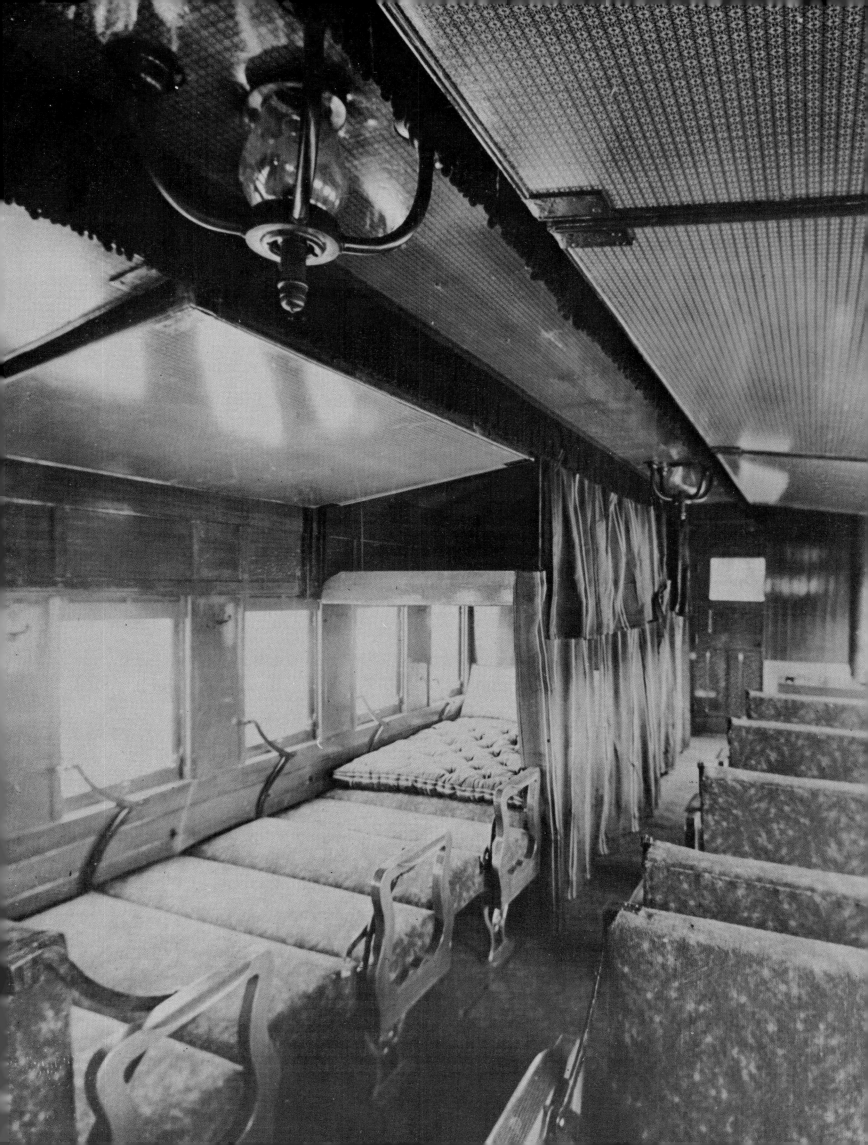

Early travellers on the transcontinental railroads met with contrasting conditions depending on their status and the fare they were able to afford. Immigrants were carried in what became known as Zulu cars (opposite, top), which provided the minimum of sleeping accommodation and were designed to be easily hosed out at the end of the journey. The introduction of the first Pullman cars on the Union Pacific (opposite) enabled wealthier travellers to enjoy a degree of comfort, and the provision of dining cars (above) proved a welcome addition to the facilities. Railroad presidents and other VIPs were able to make use of private cars equipped to the highest standards of luxury, and a special class of passenger was the royal party which accompanied the Prince of Wales on his visit to Canada in 1860. Although most of his journey was made by river, a special car was produced especially for his short rail journey (right) by the Buffalo and Lake Huron Railway.

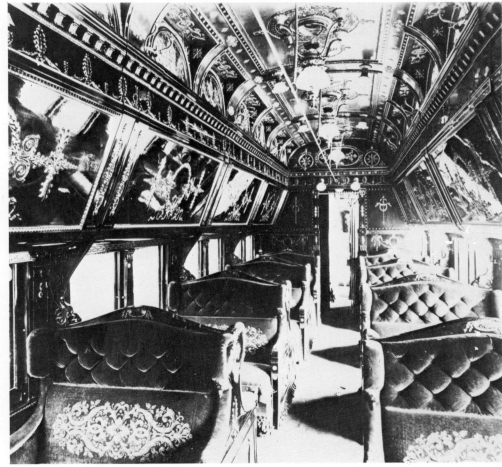

Following several early prototypes, Pullman's real breakthrough came with the construction of the *Pioneer* (left) for the Chicago and Alton Railroad. Originally rejected as too big for the line structures, the car was used to carry the body of President Lincoln back to Springfield in 1865, the line being widened to accommodate it, and the publicity attracted on that occasion was the first step towards the Pullman car's general acceptance. Most travel continued to be in standard day coaches such as those on the typical mid-century train below.

combining sleeping accommodation with a kitchen and portable tables, were built for the Great Western Railway of Canada in 1867, and in 1888 the first dining car was built for the Chicago and Alton. Luxury day coaches known as Palace Cars followed, and it was soon apparent that connection between the individual cars was desirable.

The result, in 1887, was Pullman's patented vestibuled car, which used steel springs to hold a steel-framed diaphragm over the platform at the end of one car against a similar arrangement on its neighbor. This enabled passengers to cross in safety from car to car, and also made a major contribution to safety, by helping to suppress the tendency of the platforms to ride over each other and increase the damage caused in crashes.

Thanks to the vestibuled car, the limited train, with its combination of sleeping, dining, smoking, library, bathroom and barber facilities, became fashionable; and on the long trips to the west coast passengers queued to pay the supplementary charge for Pullman service.

Nor did Pullman simply build the cars and leave them to others to operate. Each car was provided with its own attendant, punctiliously schooled in the minutiae of caring for passengers, his conduct governed by a rule book that detailed every aspect of his job. This arrangement persisted until 1947, when an antitrust suit forced the company to choose between building and operating cars. Unfortunately, the company chose to keep on building, and gave up their operation to a new consortium formed by a group of railroads. Uncertainty over the future of American passenger travel subsequently led to the company's decision to abandon the construction of the cars themselves.

Pullman's enterprise inspired a host of imitators. Many railroads built their own cars, while other organizations, such as the Woodruff and Wagner companies, were formed as specialist builders and operators. But the name of Pullman retained its magic, and over the years new designs were produced to meet changing requirements.

In 1907 the first all-steel Pullman was produced. By this time the accommodation included curtained seating

Above: Tail observation platform of the Great Northern's Oriental Limited at the turn of the century. Below: The Union Pacific M-10000T.

Right: The Centennial club car produced in the style of the 1890s for use on the Atchison, Topeka and Santa Fe's Kansas City Chief.

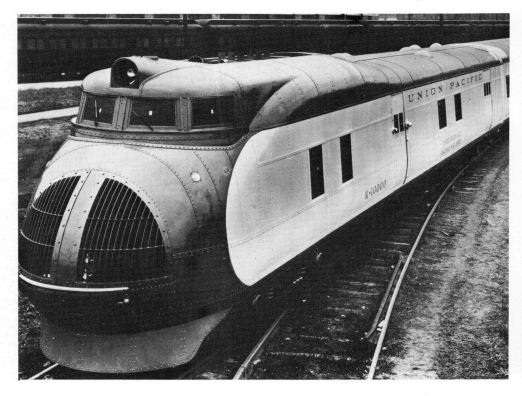

sections which could be converted to incorporate berths at night, a ladies' drawing room at one end of the car, and a gentlemen's smoking compartment at the other end. Air-conditioning was added in the late 1920s, and in the 1930s the roomette was introduced, replacing the curtained alcoves with individual compartments that combined day seating, folding berths and toilet facilities. At first 18 roomettes were contained in each car, but by staggering the position of the floors and arranging for one bed to slide underneath the higher floor and the bed in the next compartment to fold against the wall, 24 individual roomettes were packed into a single car.

Matching this improvement in accommodation was an acceleration in the speed of services. In the late nineteenth century 40-mph trains boasted names like Thunderbolt or Cannonball, but long-distance travelers were still forced inevitably to make frequent changes. Even in New York, many train journeys began with a ferry across the Hudson, since only the New York Central, with its Grand Central Station, had a terminus in the city, and the only other railroad to operate from it was the New York, New Haven and Hartford.

This latter situation, at least, was remedied in 1910 when the Pennsylvania Railroad opened its own station on Manhattan Island. One consequence of this move was to intensify competition on the route to Chicago, which in the 1890s had been covered by as many as 44 through trains daily.

Wide variation in routes led to wide variation in timings, and before the First World War, the railroads concerned agreed a standard timing of 28 hours for the journey. Since the distances involved ranged from the Pennsylvania's 902.7 miles to the Erie's 995.6 miles, it was further agreed that a supplementary charge of one dollar should be levied for each hour by which the standard time was reduced.

The leaders on the Chicago run were the Pennsylvania and the New York Central, who ran their prestige trains, the Broadway Limited and the Twentieth Century Limited, between the two cities in 18 hours, though after the war this was raised to 20 hours. Given the additional charges for the Pullman service on these trains, there was a substantial price differential between the slower services and their more famous counterparts.

To match the image of the streamlined trains of the 1930s new types of Pullman car were produced. The Duplex car of 1936 (left) included two double and 14 single sleeping compartments, and like the Roomette car of the following year (below left), which had 18 individual bedrooms, featured air-conditioning and separate heating and ventilation controls for each compartment.

Below: Interior of a bedroom on the Chicago, Burlington and Quincy's California Zephyr streamliner.

During the 1920s the accent was on service, the last word in luxury being matched by the opulence of the catering; but as the private automobile began to make its presence felt, speed was the vital factor enabling the railroads to compete in an area where they had previously enjoyed a virtual monopoly. This trend was epitomized by the introduction of the streamliners in the 1930s, for the publicity value of their spectacular appearance was a valuable weapon in the fight against the falling traffic that stemmed from the combination of economic depression and the growth of private transport.

The first streamliner was introduced by the Union Pacific, using Pullman-built aluminum cars and an early diesel engine. In 1934 this train, which went into service after a demonstration tour as the City of Salina, recorded speeds of up to 110 mph with only a 400-hp engine, so promising to combine impressive economy with a speed of service and appearance that would help lure passengers back onto the rails.

It was considered essential that the new services should bear names that would appeal to the public's imagination. The Chicago, Burlington and Quincy was one of the first railroads to operate streamliners, setting a number of trends with its Zephyr, introduced in 1934. The first Zephyr was a three-car train built by the Budd company of Philadelphia and using one of the early 600-hp Electromotive diesel engines. The first service established was between Lincoln, Nebraska, and Kansas City by way of Omaha, and passenger reaction was sufficiently encouraging for the services soon to be extended to other cities.

Nevertheless, not all the new streamliners were diesel powered. In 1935 the Milwaukee Road began operating its Hiawathas with magnificent speed-shrouded steam locomotives. The Hiawatha service was initially restricted to the highly competitive route between Chicago and Minneapolis and St Paul, but was also extended to include runs north to the shore of Lake Superior, and west to Omaha, Sioux Falls and across the continent via the Olympian Hiawatha to Spokane.

Among other western long-distance streamliners were such famous trains as the Santa Fe's Super Chief, in-

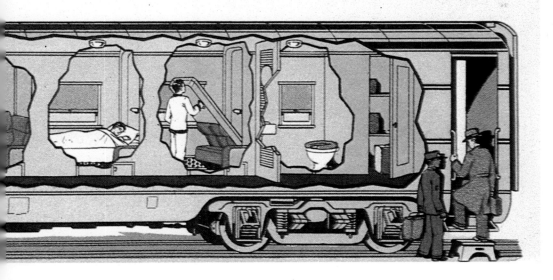

179

Above: A pair of the Burlington Route's Zephyr streamliners at Chicago in the late 1930s.

Below: Interior of the Silver Tureen, dining car of the Burlington Route's Twin Cities Zephyr.

Below: The Skytop Lounge car at the tail of a Milwaukee Road Hiawatha at Columbus in 1950.

Above: A streamlined Hudson of the New York Central with a royal train northbound at Paskill, New York.

Below: The full-length dining car of the Twentieth Century Limited introduced in 1948. With seats for 60 passengers and piped music, this car was unusual in not also containing the kitchen.

troduced in 1937 with diesel power and Pullman coaches for the marathon Chicago–Los Angeles route. Another streamliner between these two cities was the Union Pacific's City of Los Angeles, while the City of Portland and City of San Francisco served their respective cities.

One exception to the general rule of streamliners aiming for highest speeds plus finest accommodation came after the Second World War, by which time trains were facing new competition from the airlines on the longer routes. Having pioneered the high-speed concept in the 1930s, the Burlington, in 1949, introduced the domeliner, in the form of the California Zephyr. Coaches for the California service included domed observation cars specially built by Budd and intended to offer an extra ingredient to the journey by making the most of the magnificent scenery of the Far West.

The Burlington's lead was followed by a number of railroads, among them the Canadian Pacific. In Canada, of course, the transcontinental railroads really were transcontinental, and since the 1880s Canadian Pacific, with later competition from Canadian National, had run through services between Montreal and Vancouver. In 1955, Canadian Pacific introduced its own domecar train for the aptly named Canadian service.

Declining traffic affected the Canadian services, as it did every other service in later years. In 1965 Canadian National's Dominion transcontinental service was withdrawn, and in 1978, with the formation of the national VIA-Rail passenger service operation, the surviving Canadian and Canadian National's Super Continental were

Below: Interior of a lounge car on the Baltimore and Ohio Railroad's Columbian in 1957. Far left: Inside the dome car of the Columbian in 1949. Opposite: The cocktail lounge of the Atchison, Topeka and Santa Fe's Super Chief. Opposite, bottom: Dome cars enabled two levels of accommodation to be combined, with facilities such as this elegant Union Pacific dining room on the lower deck.

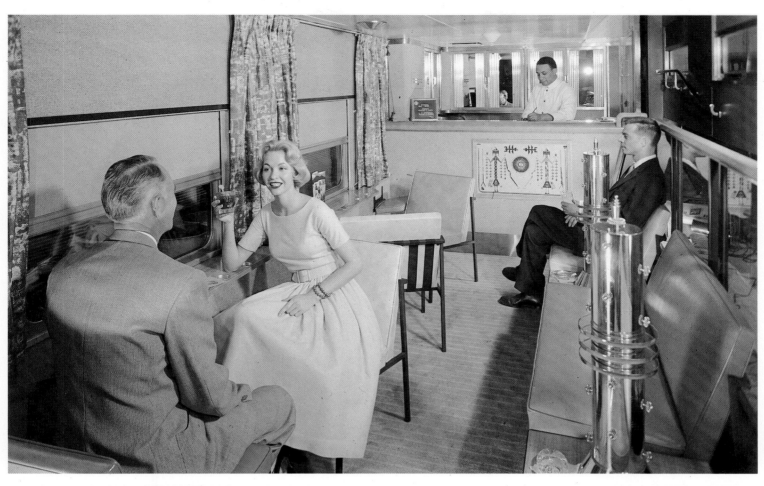

True transcontinental trains were to be found in Canada, where the Canadian Pacific introduced its Canadian service with dome cars. Page 184 shows the Canadian eastbound in the Rockies, and the upper view on page 185 is of the interior of the tail observation car on the train. Amtrak's takeover of passenger services in 1972 saw the end of many of the old named trains, but some were retained, such as the San Francisco Zephyr shown entering the High Sierras of California on page 185. The Autotrain Corporation's vacation specials to Florida, shown here, enable passengers to combine the comfort of rail travel with the convenience of the automobile.

combined over a long portion of the transcontinental route between Sudbury and Winnipeg.

In the United States, the arrival of Amtrak heralded the end of many of the famous old names. The Rio Grande persisted with its Rio Grande Zephyr between Denver and Salt Lake City, and Southern Railways kept its

Southern Crescent in service between Washington and New Orleans, with a through sleeping car service, after a night spent in the stationary sleeper, to Los Angeles; but there was not enough demand to keep many of the other services in operation.

Some of the services, however, were given new names. One of the most renowned of the old streamliners was the Southern Pacific's Coast Daylight between Los Angeles and San Francisco, nowadays replaced by the Coast Starlight, which extends along almost the whole Pacific coastline from Seattle to Los Angeles. The Hiawatha also lives on as the North Coast Hiawatha, but the vast majority of the railroads today are devoted exclusively to freight. Passenger trains are operated over only a fraction of the total track.

Moreover, timings of the modern services are substantially down on those operated during the 1950s or 1930s, though any attempt to compete with the airlines in terms of speed would be pointless over the longer routes. The main reason for the deterioration of schedules is the dilapidated state of

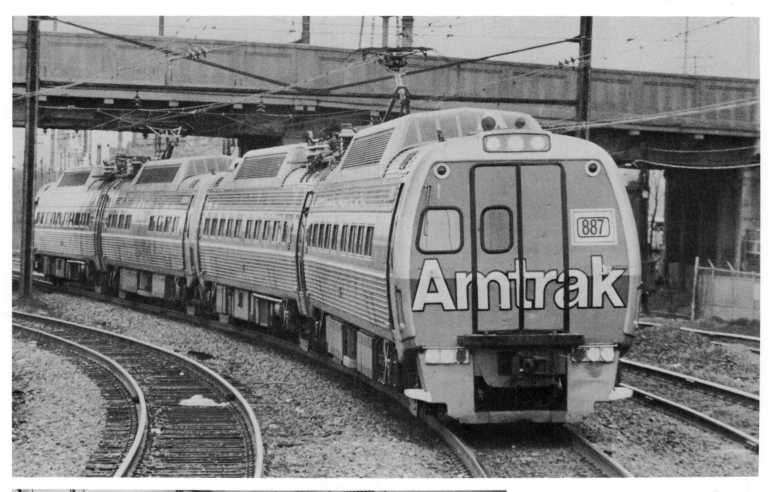

Above: One of the Budd Metroliner electric trains used by Amtrak on the northeast corridor route between New York and Washington. Left: The lower-level kitchen in the dining car of an Amtrak Superliner. Opposite top: Bi-level Superliner cars of Amtrak's Empire Builder leave Chicago en route for Seattle.

much of the track, which simply does not permit high-speed trains.

One specialized service has been established in recent years by offering a facility that no other form of transport can match. This is the Auto-Train Corporation, formed in 1969 after studies by the Ford Motor Company and federal agencies had agreed that there was a potential profit to be made from an automobile ferry service, giving passengers the comfort of long-distance train transport plus the convenience of taking their automobiles with them.

Auto-Train, having purchased sleeping cars and day coaches from a variety of railroads who had no further use for them, together with auto-carrying cars from Canadian National and new

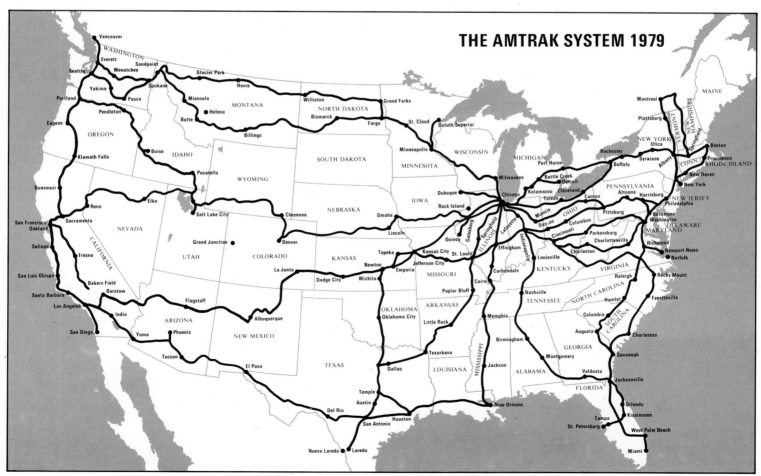

THE AMTRAK SYSTEM 1979

locomotives from General Electric, began operations in 1971 over the tracks of the Seaboard Coast Line and the Richmond, Fredericksburg and Potomac Railroad between Lorton, Virginia, and Sanford, Florida. The popularity of the holiday route to Florida enabled Auto-Train to show a healthy operating profit by the mid-1970s. Although a second service between Louisville and Sanford, operated in conjunction with Amtrak, was discontinued in 1977, another innovation was introduced together with Eastern Airlines, enabling tourists to fly to Florida and have their automobiles delivered by train.

While the prestige services inevitably attract the most attention in any review of rail travel, these have always represented only a part of the railroads' passenger operations. During the late nineteenth century, for example, there were large numbers of special immigrant trains, used to transport settlers from Europe to the new land in the west. Several of the transcontinental lines, especially those operating in the northwest, employed large numbers of agents in Europe who would advertise the attractions of the new country and arrange passage for those who were persuaded to seek their futures there.

Inevitably, conditions on many of the trains that met the new arrivals were little better than primitive. Sleeping cars were designed with wooden benches along the sides for bunks, and internally they were kept as spartan as possible so that they could be hosed down quickly at the conclusion of their journeys.

At the other end of the scale were the lavish private saloons used by the wealthiest travelers. Built to individual specifications, the only limit on what they might offer was the size of the coach and the depth of the customer's purse. The Pullman company alone built some 450 coaches for private customers before the great crash of 1929

The Amtrak North Coast Hiawatha, successor to the old Milwaukee Road service, with inset views of the Amtrak passenger depot at Richmond, Virginia, passengers boarding the Coast Starlight, and the interior of the Southwest Limited.

190

put an end to such extravagance, with prices ranging from $50,000 to seven times that amount.

Finally, there was one type of passenger that the railroads positively discouraged, since he paid no fare and preferred to avoid passenger trains altogether. The innumerable hobos who roamed the railroads became an integral part of the scene, as they followed the harvests in search of seasonal work. In fact, while some railroads discouraged free rides to the point of brakemen throwing them off moving trains, others, especially in the early days of settlement in the Far West, accepted them, knowing that without migrant laborers the crops that constituted their freight traffic would rot in the fields.

Left: The Frontier Shack tap car on the Union Pacific's City of Denver. Below. Missouri Pacific lounge car of 1936. Opposite: The Little Nugget saloon car of the Union Pacific's City of Los Angeles. Opposite, bottom: Skytop lounge on the Olympian Hiawatha.

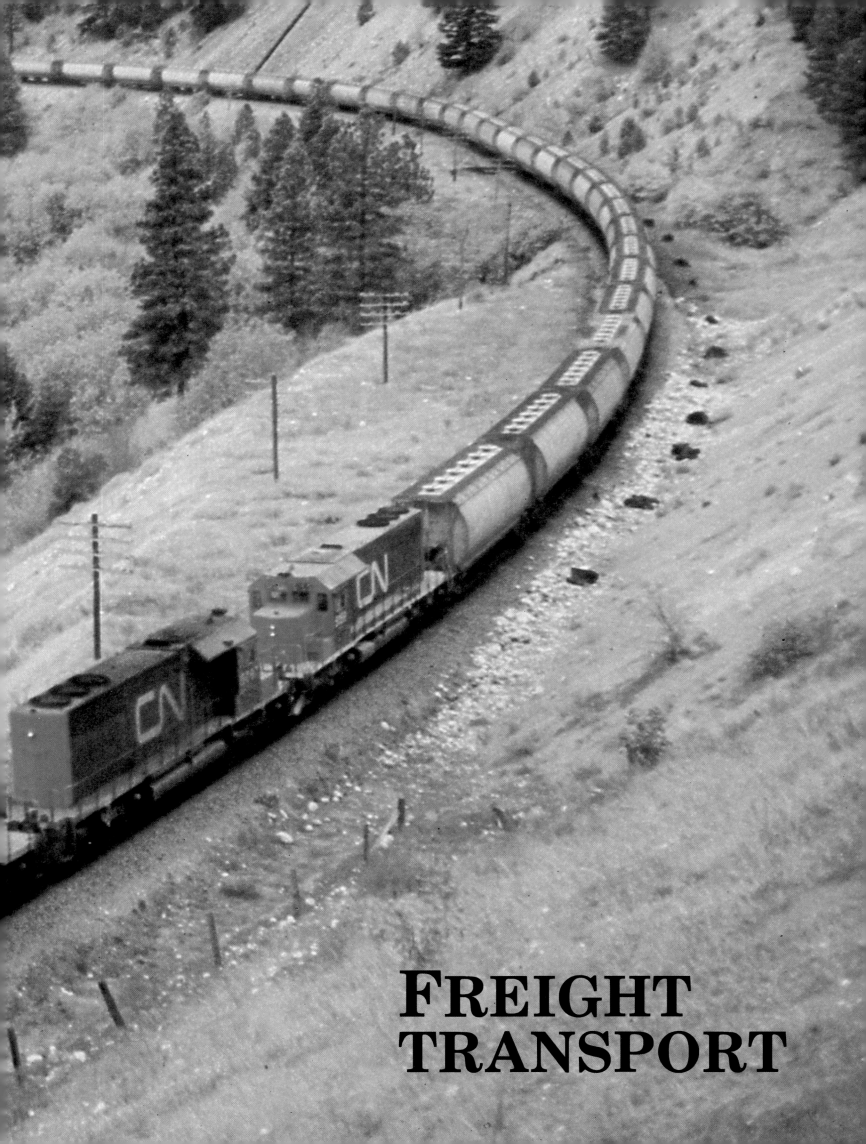

FREIGHT
TRANSPORT

efore steam locomotives were ever
thought of, railways were used to
ease the handling of heavy loads.
In quarries and mines they found their
first application, and in the United
States it was the prospect of gathering
the harvests of the west that first encouraged the builders of railroads to lay
their tracks from the east coast toward
the great rivers of the interior.

At first, it was the intention of those
builders to operate their railroads in the
same way as toll roads or canals: they
would provide the tracks, and anyone
prepared to pay the fee would be
allowed to haul their own vehicles over
them. This system was soon realized to
be impractical, however, and the
operators assumed responsibility for all
aspects of transport.

This involved the provision of suitable vehicles, the motive power to get
them to their destination, depots where
goods could be delivered, loaded, un-
loaded and collected, and a system of

**Above: An early iron ore train
crosses a lake. Right: A local mine
railroad above tracks of the
Fremont, Elkhorn and Missouri
Valley and Chicago, Burlington and
Quincy railroads in South Dakota.**

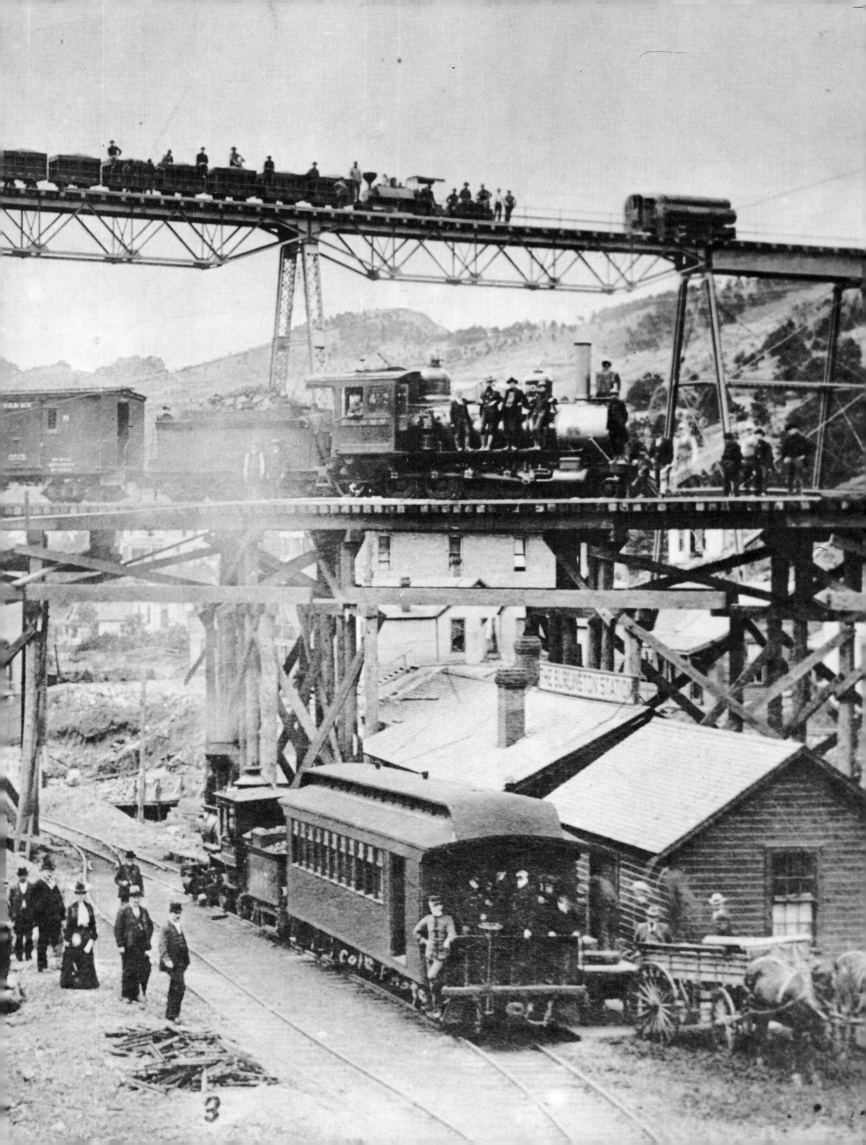

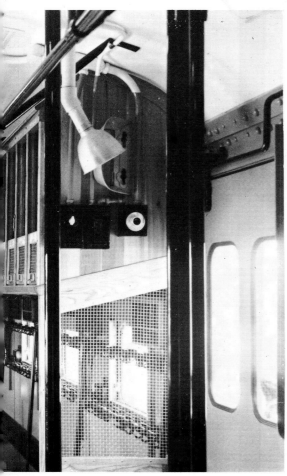

COMMUTER RAILROADS AND RAPID TRANSIT

As soon as the railroad network had provided the basis for the huge commercial and industrial growth of large cities, they began to extend the cities themselves, providing the means for the inhabitants of nearby towns to travel in daily to work in the newly established factories and businesses. Gradually, the suburban towns became absorbed by the cities, and the rail services spread further and further. At an early stage of this growth, commuter traffic became a specialized branch of railroad activity, with its own types of rolling stock and, almost as soon as it was under way, its own operational problems.

In the decades after the Civil War, railroads encouraged the growth of suburbs. Industry and the railroads were dependent on each other: industry could only grow on the strength of rail transport, and growth in industry would provide the traffic the railroads needed. The suburbs had a vital part to play in this mutual growth, providing both the workforce to operate trade and industry, and the market for its products; and the prospect of regular traffic daily over the same routes, at predictable times and in substantial numbers, must have seemed an ideal form of business to the railroad planners.

However, even before the end of the nineteenth century, it was apparent that suburban services would be beset with problems. Essentially, commuter traffic demanded large quantities of rolling stock and motive power, a sophisticated organization and a high level of efficiency, but it was utilized for only a few hours every day. Trains had to be run in both directions, but were only used by customers in one direction at a time, into the cities in the morning, and back to the suburbs at the end of the day. Furthermore, the provision of purpose-built coaches, with minimal facilities and high capacity, though enabling more passengers to be carried on each train, were useless for any other function, so that the expense of providing them – and cleaning, maintaining and storing them outside the peak hours when they were in use – dissipated the savings made by their introduction.

The situation only became worse as

The first New York elevated railway was opened in 1867, and steam locomotives were used, as in this scene in 1884, until 1903. Chicago was also early with elevated railways, the first line being opened in 1892: a 2nd Avenue train is shown (inset) at Chatham Square Station.

the years passed. The 1920s brought serious competition from the private automobile, the 1930s brought economic depression, and the Second World War was followed by a further marked decline in passenger traffic. By the 1960s commuter services were in crisis: little had been done for decades in the way of renewing equipment, and practically any development only seemed to make matters worse. Increases in fares led to a further loss of passengers; on the other hand, increase in demand for uneconomic services only meant higher losses for the railroads. New demand was stimulated by increased traffic congestion in the 1960s, but this was concentrated on the rush hour periods when services were already under pressure, and was accompanied by continuing decline in custom during the rest of the week.

At the same time, it was recognized that commuter services were essential to the continued life of cities. The inescapable fact was that public transport was a necessity that could only be provided with the assistance of large amounts of public money. There was no possibility of breaking even, let alone making a profit, with the existing pattern of commuter services, and subsidies were needed both for the renewal of obsolete equipment and to underwrite the day-to-day operating costs.

The first steps in dealing with the problem came in the 1950s with moves toward the formation of regional transportation authorities; and in 1964 the Urban Mass Transportation Act authorized federal subsidies of two-thirds of the cost of approved schemes to improve public transport. The impending collapse, near the end of the decade, of many railroads, particularly in the northeast, led to the 1970 Urban Mass Transportation Assistance Act, which increased the provision of government funds and guaranteed the existing schemes for another ten years.

The result was the creation of new transport organizations in many cities. The Metropolitan Transportation Authority covering the New York area, for example, became responsible for moving more than seven million people a day on subways, buses and the main-line railroads of the bankrupt Penn-Central and Long Island Railroads, whose services were taken over by Conrail. Conrail also found itself operating commuter services on behalf of the Boston, Philadelphia, New Jersey and Connecticut transport authorities, and in 1977 it was obliged by law to operate commuter trains for any local authority prepared to subsidize the services. Public transport authorities were also enabled to buy their own rolling stock and track, to be operated by Conrail. This has given rise to some extremely complicated services with various organizations sharing the ownership and operation of the suburban passenger trains.

At the same time as public funding of commuter services became established, renewed efforts were made to improve efficiency by the provision of new equipment. One obvious answer to the problem of increasing passenger capac-

ity without running additional trains was to use double-deck cars. In many cases, the limited length of platforms on old stations prevented any increase in the length of trains, but the near doubling of seating areas by the incorporation of an upper deck provided a useful extension of accommodation. A number of railroads had introduced such cars from the early 1950s, and their use has become increasingly common.

Some of the first double-deck cars were introduced on the Chicago, Burlington and Quincy suburban services

in the late 1940s, when steam operation was still in force. The necessity of uncoupling locomotives and turning them round for the return journey at each end of the route was a long-standing nuisance on commuter services; but it has since been overcome by the use of diesel traction. Modern commuter trains are generally operated on the push-pull principle, with a driving cab at each end of the train. Some of these trains are in fixed sets, while others are arranged so that the length can be varied according to demand, thus avoid-

Rapid transit systems are a vital factor in modern city life. Opposite, top: A train of rapid rail cars on the Chicago Transit Authority's elevated railway in 1978. Opposite, bottom: Metro Center station on the new Washington, DC, metro system, showing the driverless locomotives, in 1976. Above: Modern stainless steel R-44 subway cars for the New York City Transit Authority subways. Left: The communications controller at the Bay Area Rapid Transit control center at Lake Merritt, Oakland, from which all passenger announcements are made.

ing the expense of running unnecessarily long trains outside rush hours.

The counterpart of the commuter train, usually operating over distances of 20 miles or more from the city centers, is the shorter rapid transit line, normally confined to the inner city areas. Since these systems were built within the boundaries of established cities, they have often been forced underground in order to penetrate the busiest districts, although the first urban railway, the New York Elevated,

adopted the other possible solution and was mounted on a raised platform.

As early as 1867, a New York state committee investigating the transport needs of the city came to the conclusion that an underground railway was the only immediate solution, but the same year saw the opening of the first section of elevated railway. Initial experiments with cable traction were soon discarded in favor of the use of steam locomotives. Further experiments followed with pneumatic power, but steam locomotives remained in operation on the

growing network of elevated lines until 1903, when electric traction took over completely.

By this point the first subways were under construction, and in 1904 the first underground line, running just over nine miles from City Hall via Grand Central Station to Times Square and Broadway at 145th Street, was inaugurated. Subways and elevated railways were also built in Chicago, Philadelphia and Boston around the turn of the century, but it was some years before other cities followed suit.

Chicago's first subway was brought into operation in 1943, and Cleveland opened its short rapid transit line, most of which is on the surface, in 1955.

Recent years, with growing traffic congestion, have forced other North American cities to consider plans for rapid transit railways, but the enormous cost of tunneling under city centers has caused many to be postponed, and others to be revised to use light rail systems instead. Toronto and Montreal opened the first stages of expanding rapid transit systems in 1954 and 1966 respectively.

Meanwhile, two new rapid transit systems have been started. The first is the Bay Area Rapid Transit system in the San Francisco district, opened to the public in 1972 after 26 years of discussion, planning and construction. Despite such a long gestation period, however, the B.A.R.T. system's wholesale adoption of the latest technology has led to many operating problems and a degree of cost escalation which can hardly have encouraged other cities planning their own systems.

The first schemes for a rapid transit railway to connect San Francisco, Oakland and Berkely were put forward in 1946 as an alternative to the increasing traffic congestion, especially on the bridges across San Francisco Bay; but it was not until 1957 that the Bay Area Rapid Transit District Authority was established. A plan produced in 1961 was then further delayed because of objections from taxpayers and controversy over the proposed route, but the 1964 Urban Mass Transportation Act came to the rescue with federal subsidies.

The B.A.R.T. system was planned to use the most modern techniques in every area, from construction that involved a three-and-a-half-mile prefabricated tunnel being laid across the bed of San Francisco Bay, to operation, with 80-mph electric train sets under full computer control and tickets dispensed by automatic fare-collection machines.

In service, however, the B.A.R.T. system has experienced every conceivable problem, with revision of everything from ticket machines to the cushions used in the cars, and the computer operation having to be supplemented by

station dispatchers while a new signaling arrangement was installed.

The other new rapid transit system, which benefited both from the Urban Mass Transportation Act and the experience of the B.A.R.T. operators, is the Washington, D.C., Metro. Construction of the Washington Metro began in 1969, and the first section of a planned 101-mile system was opened in 1976. The teething troubles of the Metro have been on nothing like the same scale as those of B.A.R.T., although it also uses computers to control its operations.

A major consideration in the planning of the Metro system was its integration into an overall transport policy. One facet of this is the basic need to attract customers, and the carpeted, air-conditioned cars are complemented by spacious, air-conditioned stations whose design has been calculated to minimize crime. At the same time, the suburban stations, of which there are 34 compared with the 53 in the central area, are provided with substantial parking areas and large forecourts to encourage switching from automobile to train for the journey to the city center, and bus routes have been reworked to connect with Metro stations.

Naturally, the cost of such advanced systems is enormous. However, the alternative of constructing ever-increasing numbers of urban expressways and flooding city centers with more and more automobiles is hardly a realistic solution to the problem of inner city transport needs. It seems clear that railroads, in one form or another, are the most promising method of transporting large numbers of people, especially over the heavily used urban routes. It is equally clear that public funding is required to provide the huge capital costs of building new systems or modernizing existing ones, but the savings offered by automation may well offset the initial costs to the extent that new railroads will come to be seen as a bargain.

The Montreal metro station at Berri-de-Montigny, part of the system opened in 1967 which uses rubber-tired trains. Inset: Upper deck of a bi-level suburban coach of the Government of Ontario's Toronto Area Transit Operating Authority.

INDEX

The publishers and researchers would like to thank the following individuals and organisations who supplied illustrations for this book. For reasons of space alone, some references have been abbreviated as follows:

Association of American Railroads, Washington DC = AAR
Atchison, Topeka & Santa Fe Railway, Chicago = SF
Baltimore & Ohio Raiload = B & O
BBC Hulton Picture Library = BBC
Burlington Northern Railroad = BN
Canadian Pacific Railroad =CP
Mechanical Archive & Research Services, London = MARS
Union Pacific Railroad Museum, Nebraska = UP

Front cover: V Goldberg. Back cover: UP. p1: UP. 2–3: Gammell. 4–5: SF. 6–11 (top): B & O. 11 (btm): AAR. 12: MARS. 12–13: Gulf Oil/ARR. 13: MARS. 14–15: Western Americana Picture Library, London. 16–17: B & O. 17: MARS. 18: B & O. 19: AAR. 20–27: MARS. 28–29: UP. 30–31: Southern Pacific RR. 32–33: UP. 34–35: SF. 36–37: UP. 38: Southern Pacific Railroad. 38–39: UP. 39: : UP. 40–41: BN. 42–43: UP. 44–45: MARS. 46–47: BN. 48–49: BN. 50–51: BN. 52: BBC. 52–53: GF Allen. 54–55: B & O. 56–57: BN. 58–59: UP. 59–60: MARS. 62–63: UP. 63 (top): UP. 63 (btm): AAR. 64–65: MARS. 66–67: UP. 68: BN. 69: SF. 70–71: GF Allen. 72–73: Missouri Pacific Railraod. 74–75: GF Allen. 76: GF Allen. 76–77: C & O Railroad. 78–79: RH Kindig. 79: Milwaukee Road. 80: SF. 80–81: UP. 85: GF Allen. 86–87: J Jarvis. 88–89: Amtrak Corp. 90–91: CP. 92–93: Confederation Life. 94–95: BBC. 96: CP. 96–97: CP. 97: BBC. 99–106 (top): CP. 106 (btm): Via Rail. 107: Canadian National. 108–109: CP. 110–111: B & O. 112–113: MARS. 114–115: CP. 116: UP. 116–117: US National Archives. 117. Southern Pacific RR. 118: J Winkley. 119: UP. 120: CP. 120–121: CP. 121: BN. 122: CP. 122: CP. 123: BN. 124 (top): SF. 125: BBC. 125 (top): SF. 125 (btm): MARS. 126–127: UP. 128–129: SF. 130–131: J Jarvis. 132–133: MARS. 132: AAR. 134: J Winkley. 135: B & O. 136 (top): CP. 136 (btm): PB Whitehouse. 136–137: GF Allen. 137: AAR. 138–139: J Jarvis. 140–141: SF. 141: B & O. 142: J Jarvis. 143 (top): J Winkley. 143 (btm): M Whitehouse. 144: Norfolk & Western Railway. 145: UP. 146–147: J Winkley. 148–149: BBC. 150 (top): BN. 150 (btm): US National Archives. 151 (top): BN. 151 (btm): GF Allen. 152–153: GF Allen. 154: BN. 154–155: AAR. 156–157: UP. 158 (top): B & O. 158 (btm): J Jarvis. 159 (top): SF. 159 (btm): BN. 160 (top): SF. 160 (btm): Missouri Pacific Railroad. 161 (top): UP. 161 (btm): Chicago & North Western. 162: Via Rail. 163–165: Amtrak. 166–167: Autotrain Corp. 168–169: AAR. 169: MARS. 170: Pullman Standard. 171–173 (top): Up. 173 (btm): Canadian National/MARS. 174–175 (top): Pullman Standard. 174–175 (btm): 176 (top): BN. 176 (btm): Aluminum Company of America. 176–177: SF. 178–179: Pullman Standard. 179: AAR. 180 (top): AAR. 180 (btm): BN. 180–181: Milwaukee Road. 181 (btm): B & O. 183: SF. 184: CP. 185 (top): CP. 185 (btm): Amtrak. 186–187: Autotrain Corp. 188–191: Amtrak. 192 (top): UP. 192 (btm): GFA. 193 (top): UP. 193 (btm): Milwaukee Road. 194–195: Canadian National. 196–197: Chicago & North Western Railway. 198 (top): Southern Pacific. 198 (btm): B & O. 199: BN. 200 (top): BN. 200 (btm): SF. 201: BN. 202–203: CN. 206: BN. 207: CP. 208: Missouri Pacific. 209 (top): Illinois Gulf Central. 209 (btm). SF. 210–211: SF. 212: SF. 212–213: UP. 213: SF. 214–215: NY City Transit Authority. 216–217: BBC. 218 (top): Boeing Vertol/MARS. 218 (btm): WMATA/MARS. 219 (top): NY City Transit Authority. 219 (btm): Bay Area Rapid Transit. 220–221: Montreal Metro. 221: Hawker Siddeley Canada.